That's a Bullseye

by
Richard Blazevich
& Eric Bishop

Signal Tower Publishing
Dallas, Texas and Cincinnati, Ohio

That's a Bullseye

by
Richard Blazevich and Eric Bishop

This book is a work of fiction. Names, characters, places, and incidents are either the product of the authors' imaginations or are used fictitiously. Any resemblance to any person, living or dead, business establishments, events, or locales is entirely coincidental.

This book is protected under the copyright laws of the United States of America. Any reproductions or other unauthorized use of the material or artwork herein is prohibited without the express written permission of one of the authors.

Cover artwork of dartboard from ccPixs.com

Cover designed by Mercedes Piñera (www.behance.net/espacio_M)

Book edited by Trisha Alcisto (www.trishaalcisto.me) and qdmerit (www.fiver.com/qdmerit)

Audiobook narrated by Chris Abernathy (www.AbernathyVoice.com)

Copyright © 2017 by Richard Blazevich and Eric Bishop
All rights reserved.

Signal Tower Publishing
Dallas, Texas and Cincinnati, Ohio

Introduction

This book is a business fable. It is a fictional story about Jim Harrison, a marketing leader who joins a struggling company. He follows these steps to transform the company into a successful business with strong online sales:

1. Identify the Problems to Solve
2. Research Four Key Questions
3. Define the Current Customer Journey
4. Design a Better Experience
5. Build a Minimally Viable Product
6. Launch the Online Store and Campaign

You can use these steps to improve the performance of any organization, whether it's a for-profit business, a non-profit institution, or any other type of entity.

We wrote this story based on our combined forty plus years of experience in consumer products companies and marketing agencies. Through this story, we provide practical examples to help you engage customers, clients, donors, volunteers, or anyone else you want to attract.

We have included a list of characters at the end of the book to help you keep track of the roles that each person plays in this story.

We hope you enjoy this story and find the lessons useful to your own situation.

Contents

Step 1: Identify the Problems to Solve 1
   1. What's Wrong, Honey? 3
   2. The Premier Way of Doing Business 4
   3. No One Asked Me 6
   4. The Parking Lot Was Empty 8
   5. There Won't Be a Company Left 10
   6. He Assumed He Had No Choice 11
   7. All Hell Broke Loose 13
   8. Tell Me What the Problems Are 17

Step 2: Research Four Key Questions 19
   1. Shouldn't We Ask a Few Questions? 21
   2. What Products Should We Focus On? 25
   3. Who Makes the Purchase Decisions? 29
   4. Why Would People Choose Those Products? 32
   5. Where Do They Buy Those Products? 36
   6. There's Gonna Be a Shoot-out! 37

Step 3: Define the Current Customer Journey 39
   1. Start with the Customer Journey 41
   2. What Triggers a Purchase? 44
   3. How Do You Learn About New Brands? 46
   4. Where Do You Go to Get More Information? 47
   5. What Causes You to Purchase? 48
   6. What Can Ensure a Re-Purchase? 50

Step 4: Design a Better Experience 53
1. What Should We Call Our Brand? 55
2. Use a "Get, To, By, Because" Framework 58
3. We Should Have Debates Like This 59
4. Get Reactions from our Target Audience 62
5. Let's See Some Advertising Ideas 64
6. Stop Talking and Start Doing 66

Step 5: Build a Minimally Viable Product 69
1. We Need to Hire an Agency 71
2. All in Favor, Say Aye 73
3. When Can You Start? 78
4. Today, We'll Design Our Online Store 82
5. Let's Do an A-B Test 84
6. Just Stay out of Our Way 88
7. We Have a Revolution on Our Hands 91
8. We Need Real Users to Test the Site 93

Step 6: Launch the Online Store and Campaign 95
1. We'll Design Our Media Network 97
2. Every Star Has to Start Somewhere 100
3. That's a Bullseye 103
4. Even a Blind Squirrel Finds a Nut 106
5. We Didn't Get the $5 Million 108

Conclusion 115

Marketing Journey Templates 121
- Problems to Solve Statements.............................121
- The What, Who, Why, and Where 122
- Customer Journey 124
- Shopping Funnel 126
- Request-for-Proposal Brief..................................128
- Get, To, By, Because Brief...................................130
- Design Process 131

List of Characters 133
Acknowledgements.....................................135
About the Authors......................................136

Step 1: Identify the Problems to Solve

1. What's Wrong, Honey?

Exasperated, Jim pulled into the driveway of his large, suburban home and sat in his car. Thoughts swirled through his head as he wondered how he would tell his wife that he'd made the biggest mistake of his career.

After a few minutes of stalling, he summoned the courage to go inside. When he walked in, Sarah's voice greeted him from the kitchen. "Hey honey. Dinner'll be ready in five."

He walked past her in the kitchen, poured himself a drink, and went to the family room where he collapsed into his favorite chair. A few minutes later, he heard, "Dinner's ready." Soon after, Sarah came into the room and found him slumped over with his head in his hands.

"What's wrong, honey?" she asked. She was trying, unsuccessfully, to not sound panicked.

Jim's mind was still sorting through the events of the past few weeks. It all started when he accepted an offer for his dream job at Premier Sporting Goods. He had become their new chief marketing officer leading his own department.

He accepted the job because Premier was one of the most prestigious companies in the country, and he'd loved their products since he was a kid. Jim had moved his family to a new city, despite their objections, for the promise of a higher income and a better career. Since then, everything had gone horribly wrong.

Within a few days of joining Premier, he started noticing the telltale signs of a struggling company. Circumstances had gotten progressively worse until today, when the situation seemed completely hopeless. Now, he might have to start looking for another job.

2. The Premier Way of Doing Business

A few weeks earlier, Jim's arrived at Premier's headquarters for his first day of work. Ed Baxter, the company's chief executive officer, invited him to the monthly leadership team meeting. In the company's luxurious conference room, Ed told his team the story about his father founding the company over fifty years earlier. The other executives had heard the story many times before, but Ed wanted them to hear it again.

"For decades, we've been the best sporting goods company in the country," Ed proudly stated. "We have three pillars that have led to our success. First, the strongest relationships with all the top retailers. We have over 200 highly-experienced sales people calling on retail giants including Titan Supercenters, MegaSports Incorporated, and Behemoth Athletic Supply. Those retailers give us the best display locations in their stores, and that leads to strong year-after-year sales.

"Second, we have sponsorship agreements with legendary athletes. Our consumers choose our brands because their idols choose our brands. As long as we keep those athletes on our payroll, our competitors can't build credibility with our consumers.

"And finally, our product quality is unmatched. Through decades of refinement, we've created the perfect designs for football, baseball, and golf equipment. Those sports are the foundation of our country's athletic system, and we're dominating the market for all three."

His leadership team applauded and smiled at the mention of "dominating the market."

"Now, let me introduce the newest member of our leadership team. Jim Harrison is joining us from Smitty's Auto

Parts where he was their head of marketing. He has outstanding experience in the three areas of marketing we value most: retail marketing, sports sponsorships, and product innovation. Please join me in welcoming Jim to our team."

One by one, the executives walked up to Jim, shook his hand, and introduced themselves. The group included the heads of finance, sales, and operations. Jim noticed that, at forty-five years old, he must have been the youngest executive in the room by at least ten years.

After everyone dispersed, Jim and Ed moved into Ed's expansive office. "Jim, I'm looking forward to you carrying on our tradition of marketing success," Ed said as he handed Jim a piece of paper. "Here's your schedule for the week. As you see, you'll spend time with each member of my leadership team getting to know the Premier way of doing business."

On the paper, Ed had written the following:

Monday, 11 a.m. - Ed Baxter, Chief Executive Officer
Monday, 2 p.m. - Francis Baxter, Chief Financial Officer
Tuesday, 11 a.m. - Sam Baxter, Chief Sales Officer
Wednesday, 9 a.m. - Olivia Whitten, Chief Operations Officer

As Jim looked at the schedule, he was reminded that this was a family business. Three of the executives shared the Baxter last name, which was also the last name of the company's founder. Other than Jim, the only executive who didn't have the Baxter name was Olivia Whitten. Jim was eager to learn how she had become part of the company.

3. No One Asked Me

At 2 p.m., Jim walked into the office of Francis Baxter. "Good afternoon, Francis," he said as he glanced around the office. Jim immediately noticed a huge portrait with a gold plaque that read "Francis Baxter, Chief Financial Officer, Premier Sporting Goods."

"Have a seat," Francis said, straightening his tie as he sat behind the largest wooden desk that Jim had ever seen.

"Let's get started," Francis said as he handed Jim several sheets of paper. "Here are some reports that show how the company is doing. As you can see, we have over $200 million in sales, and we're highly profitable.

"Since we're planning to take the company public next year, profit margins are critical. We're doing everything we can to ensure we have the highest margins in the industry."

As Jim scanned the numbers, he noticed the company's profit margin was almost double that of his previous company. He was impressed.

"Do you have any historical reports?" Jim asked. "I'd like to see the sales trends to better understand the business."

"You'll have to get that from Jenny Ross, your marketing analyst." Francis pulled back the cuff of his shirt sleeve and looked at his watch. "Oh goodness, look at the time. I have a very important phone call in exactly five minutes. I must prepare." Francis stood up and walked Jim to the hallway. "If you need anything else, Jenny can answer your questions." Francis closed his office door before Jim could respond.

Puzzled, Jim stood in the hallway. He wasn't expecting such an abrupt end to the meeting. Since he still had questions, he went looking for Jenny.

As Jim walked through the area outside his office, he noticed a small cubicle with the nameplate *Jenny Ross* on it. He glanced into the cubicle and saw a young woman seated with her back to him.

"Jenny?" he said in a soft voice. No response. "Jenny?" he said a little louder. Still no response. When he stepped into the cubicle so she could see him, she nearly jumped out of her chair.

"Sorry. You startled me," she said as she reached up to her ears and removed a tiny pair of earbuds. "You must be James Harrison, our new CMO."

"That's me. Call me Jim. Sorry to interrupt. I didn't realize you were listening to something."

"Yeah, it's just a marketing podcast. I like to listen to it while I'm working on our weekly sales reports. What can I do for you?"

"I'd like to schedule some time with you to go through our historical sales numbers. Francis said you'd be the best person for that."

"How's right now?" Jenny asked in a cheerful voice.

Since Jim's meeting with Francis ended so quickly, he had plenty of time. He accepted Jenny's offer.

She pointed to a small chair where Jim could sit, and she started opening spreadsheets on her laptop. "How far back do you want to go?" she asked. "I have about ten years of data."

"Let's look at the full ten years." As Jim read through the numbers, he noticed a big sales spike about five years ago, then declining sales ever since. "What caused that increase five years ago?"

"That's when we launched our new line of soccer equipment. It didn't last long, but it sold well while we had it."

"Why didn't it last?"

"Mr. Baxter didn't like it since it had lower margins than our other products," Jenny said.

"Which Mr. Baxter?" Jim asked.

"There's only one Mr. Baxter . . . our CFO, Francis Baxter. The other Baxters go by their first names, but Francis prefers to be called Mr.," Jenny said with a little smirk.

"Was the soccer equipment profitable?"

"Yeah, but it wasn't as profitable as the other items we sell. Sam didn't like it either since it took display space away from his favorite products, the football equipment. He calls soccer a *girly sport,* so he was happy to get out of it. I would have kept the soccer stuff, but of course, no one asked me."

Jim thanked Jenny and went back to his office. He wondered what kind of company would discontinue a profitable line of equipment for a popular sport like soccer. Later, he realized that this had been a warning sign of what he had gotten himself into.

4. The Parking Lot Was Empty

On Jim's second day of work, he met Premier's head of sales, Sam Baxter, at the largest sporting goods store that Jim had ever seen. As he pulled into the parking lot, Jim noticed it was nearly empty. Even though it was a Tuesday, he had expected to see a few people shopping there, especially since kids were out of school for the summer.

Sam guided Jim around the store, pointing to giant displays of Premier football helmets, baseball bats, and golf clubs. Sam explained that each Premier salesperson had a budget for entertaining store managers which included plenty of money for fancy dinners and tickets for sporting events. "In exchange for our taking care of them, these store managers give us whatever space we ask for."

Jim paused to watch a father and son in the football aisle. He overheard the father say, "This is the type of ball I played with when I was your age. I remember TV commercials with Roger Garrett talking about how he loved the performance of Premier footballs."

"Roger who?" asked the boy, who was about ten years old. "Dad, I don't even like football. Can we check out the hoverboards? I wanna see if they have any that light up when you ride 'em."

"Hoverboards? You won't get any exercise riding hoverboards."

"But Blazer Blaze does some amazing hoverboard tricks in his YouTube videos. I wanna learn to do tricks like him."

"Look, if you're not interested in real sports, I'm not gonna bother," the dad said as he stormed toward the exit.

Jim was just as befuddled as the boy's father had been. How could the kid not appreciate the same brand of football that Roger Garrett used? As a student of the game, Jim thought every boy should learn to admire the legends of football.

When Jim got home that night, he asked his fifteen-year-old son Jake about Blazer Blaze. Jake's face lit up. "Blazer Blaze is the coolest! He has over 10 million subscribers, and some of his videos get over 100 million views. He does some crazy stuff on hoverboards, and he's one of the best parkour guys in the world."

"What's parkour?" Jim asked.

"Wow, Dad, you really are out of touch," Jake said. "Parkour is when people run through obstacles, jumping and flipping as they go. It's kinda like doing skateboard tricks without a skateboard."

"Does Blazer Blaze play football?"

Jake laughed. "Dad, no one plays football anymore."

5. There Won't Be a Company Left

On Wednesday morning, Jim went to meet Olivia Whitten, the company's head of operations. When he glanced into her office, he noticed simple, tasteful furniture throughout the room.

Olivia was saying good-bye to someone on the phone, and she waved at Jim to come into her office. As she hung up, she said, "Jim, it's good to see you again. How are your first few days going?"

"It's been very interesting," Jim replied.

"How so?"

"Honestly, I didn't realize how narrow our product line is. It seems like everything is focused on just three sports."

"I know. I've tried to get my brothers to agree to launch other products, but they won't listen to me."

"Your brothers?" Jim asked in surprise.

"Yes. Whitten is my married name. I was originally a Baxter," she said, lowering her head. She immediately perked back up. "Maybe you could help me convince them to launch something new."

"I'd like that," Jim replied with a smile.

They spent the next two hours talking about the company's research, development, and product supply processes. Jim learned that the company's approach was to slowly refine products over time, looking for ways to cut costs while maintaining quality.

Their supply chain was focused on shipping products from manufacturers in China to Premier's warehouses in the United States. Then, they would ship those products to big, brick-and-mortar retailers across the country. They didn't have any online sales, and they had no plans to expand into new product lines.

"We've gotten very comfortable with our existing business model," Olivia said with a hint of disappointment. "Every time I've tried to get my brothers to do something new, Francis and Sam remind me what a hassle it was when we launched our line of soccer equipment. They have no interest in going through that again."

"I've looked at the company's sales numbers," Jim said, "and I'm worried. If we don't do something soon, there won't be a company left."

"I know. I just can't seem to get through to my brothers."

Jim left Olivia's office relieved that someone else recognized the problems the company was facing, but he was discouraged that the other executives seemed complacent. What was he going to do?

6. He Assumed He Had No Choice

That afternoon, Jim met with Patrick Feldman, VP of Sports Sponsorships and the most senior member of Jim's marketing team.

Patrick explained that they spent most of their marketing budget on sponsorship deals with top football, baseball, and golf athletes. "We have very strict guidelines for the athletes we sponsor," Patrick explained. "Each athlete must have at least five years of professional experience in their sport, and must have won at least one championship during their career."

Jim asked, "Would we ever sponsor a rookie?"

"Never!" Patrick shook his head and scoffed. "Rookies don't have the credibility that veterans have. Plus, you can't trust rookies. You never know when they'll do something stupid and end up in jail.

"Now, let me tell you about the deal we're working on with Walt Bigman." Patrick explained that they were planning to pay the famous football player $5 million next year, which would include two TV commercials and ten personal appearances.

"We typically use the personal appearances for meetings with our top retail partners," Patrick said. "They love hanging out with their sports heroes. It makes 'em feel important.

"We're worried about getting into a bidding war with Legacy Athletics, our biggest competitor. We can't afford lose to them. It wouldn't be good for you if they got Walt."

"Wouldn't be good for me?" Jim asked.

Patrick shrugged. "You're our deal-maker. I just do the paperwork. It's on you to close the deal."

Jim went to his office and wondered if he really wanted to spend $5 million dollars on one athlete sponsorship. Since that was his job, he assumed he had no choice.

7. All Hell Broke Loose

Over the next few weeks, Jim settled into his new role. He noticed that the company was split into two groups: the *old guard* who was comfortable with business as usual and the *newbies* who wanted to change things but were usually overruled.

Whenever a tough decision needed to be made, it would go to Francis and Sam Baxter. They would take whichever path fit their conservative business approach. When Ed was informed, he wouldn't push back on anything Francis and Sam wanted. He was so pre-occupied with taking the company public that he wasn't getting involved in the day-to-day business decisions.

On the day that all hell broke loose, Jim was in the conference room with the other executives. He was giving his first monthly marketing update and presenting ideas for a digital advertising campaign.

"I think these are great ideas," Olivia said with enthusiasm. "The digital ads will help us reach younger consumers. Love it."

"What? No." Sam sat back in his chair, looking from Olivia to Jim. "Sorry Jim. It'll never work. Our retail customers will hate it. If we redirect our marketing budget away from athlete sponsorships to digital media . . . No. We're not risking our credibility for that."

"I agree with Sam," Francis said. "These are terrible ideas. A digital marketing campaign would cost way too much. We just don't have that kind of money, especially with the $5 million contract for Bigman. That alone will wipe out our marketing budg-."

A knock on the conference room door drew everyone's attention to Patrick Feldman. He slowly opened the door and stepped in with an apologetic expression on his face. "Sorry guys, but you'll want to see this." He dropped a newspaper on the conference table so everyone could read the headline: "WALT BIGMAN SIGNS DEAL WITH ZOOM SPORTS FOR $3MM IN STOCK."

"What?" Sam stood up and pounded his fist on the table. "Who the hell is Zoom Sports, and why didn't you prevent this, Jim? This is going to kill us!"

Francis picked up the newspaper and flung it across the table. "This is devastating! Without that contract, our total financial model is blown for the year."

Jim's mind went blank. He was in complete shock. He had secretly dreamed that this deal wouldn't go through so he could use the money for other projects. But now that the deal had fallen apart, he realized it could be devastating for his career.

Sam shouted, "Jim, get the hell out of here! You need to find a way to kill Walt's deal with Zoom and get him back on board with us."

Patrick shook his head. "It can't be done. Our lawyer is the one who showed me the article. He said Walt's contract with Zoom forbids him from doing sponsorships with any other sporting goods companies. Our deal with Walt is dead."

Francis turned to Jim. "If you'd spent more time with Walt instead of on those idiotic digital ideas, this never would have happened!"

Olivia came to Jim's defense. "Guys, c'mon. This may be good news. Now we can use that $5 million for something else . . . like online ads or a new line of products."

Sam ignored Olivia and blurted out, "Jim, go figure out how to make this right, or start looking for another job."

Jim excused himself from the room and retreated to his office.

About twenty minutes later, Jim heard an announcement on the overhead speaker. "All executives report to the Leadership Conference Room for an emergency meeting." *Oh no.* They were going to announce that Jim would be fired. He took one look around his office and slowly walked to the conference room.

When he entered, no one made eye contact with him. Ed cleared his throat and told everyone to sit down. "It's a very sad day for our company. We've had a major setback that will be very difficult to overcome."

"I know," Sam said. "Without Walt, we're screwed!"

"No, I'm not talking about Walt," Ed said. That got Jim's attention. What could be worse than losing Walt? "Our investment bankers just informed me that Titan Supercenters is declaring bankruptcy. Since they represent 40% of our sales, we might need to do some serious restructuring. The investment bankers are postponing our initial public offering, at least until we can show them how we'll make up for the lost sales."

"What?" Francis turned on Sam. "Why didn't you tell us about this? You just played golf with Titan's CEO on Saturday. Why would you hide this from us?"

Sam looked around the room. "He didn't mention anything about it. He seemed fine on Saturday. I don't understand."

"Well," Francis replied, "I guess your relationship with him wasn't as good as you said it was."

The executives spent the rest of the day trying to figure out what they were going to do. Finally, Ed announced, "That's it for today. We all need a break. I want everyone to go home, get some rest, and start coming up with better ideas. My next meeting with the investment bankers is only four months away, so we'll need some very specific plans by then."

As Jim walked out of the conference room, Jenny Ross motioned him over with a wave. "Jenny, not now."

"This can't wait. Patrick was looking for you, but I told him you were in a meeting. He handed me this and walked out."

Jim looked a piece of paper from Jenny's hand. It was short and to the point.

> *Dear Mr. Harrison,*
>
> *I hereby submit my resignation. I am going to pursue other interests.*
>
> *Since I have 2 weeks of vacation that I haven't taken yet, I will not be returning to the office until I take those 2 weeks. At the end of that time, I will return and collect my final paycheck.*
>
> *Sincerely,*
> *Patrick Feldman*

What a mess! Jim politely thanked Jenny, grabbed his jacket from his office, and went straight to his car. As he drove home, he wondered how he ended up in a company with steadily declining sales and a portfolio of products that were losing relevance with consumers.

Exasperated, Jim pulled into the driveway of his large, suburban home and sat in his car. Thoughts swirled through his head as he wondered how he would tell his wife that he'd made the biggest mistake of his career.

8. Tell Me What the Problems Are

"What's wrong, honey?" Sarah asked, sounding even more worried the second time. When Jim didn't answer, she pushed him gently. "Hey, answer me! What's wrong?"

After a long pause, Jim whispered, "This company is a disaster. What have I gotten us into?"

"What do you mean?" Sarah asked.

"People aren't buying our products, which means our business is in bad shape."

"Well that's obvious. All you sell is stuff for sports that kids aren't playing anymore."

"What?" Jim looked at his wife with disbelief. "How long have you known that?"

"Since your first week, when you had that conversation with Jake at the dinner table. He told you that kids his age aren't playing football. They're into other things."

"Why didn't you say anything?"

"Well, you're the expert," she replied. "I thought you already knew. You're working on a plan to fix it, aren't you?"

"Uh . . . I am now. I'm just not sure where to start."

"Oh." She took a slow breath and changed her approach. "How about you tell me exactly what the problems are?"

"I've already told you. The company is a wreck, our sales are declining, and our marketing isn't working."

"Okay, that's a start. Now, what's the cause?"

"Well, our products aren't as popular as they used to be, and we're not selling our products in the right places."

"Hold that thought," Sarah said. She got up, went to the kitchen, and came back a minutes later with a small piece of paper. She handed it to Jim. "Here, put this somewhere you'll see it every day," she said. "That way, when you look at it, you'll know what to focus on."

Three short lines were written in Sarah's neat handwriting.

> PROBLEMS TO SOLVE:
> 1. Products aren't relevant
> 2. Products aren't sold where people shop

Jim stared at the list and looked at his wife. He responded cautiously. "Alright . . ." He knew she was trying to help. "But where do I start?"

Sarah paused for a moment, then said, "Why don't you ask the people who work for you? Can't they help?"

"But it's my job to make the decisions. I'm the one who's supposed to have the answers, not my staff."

"Okay, big shot," Sarah said with a grin. "So you're supposed to walk into a company with all the answers and tell the people who've worked there for years what they should be doing. Wouldn't they have better ideas since they know the business?"

"If they had better ideas, don't you think they would have said something by now?"

"Not necessarily. Maybe no one ever asked 'em for ideas. Why don't you ask 'em? What do you have to lose?"

Step 2: Research Four Key Questions

1. Shouldn't We Ask a Few Questions?

The next morning, Jim hosted his weekly staff meeting. When everyone settled into the conference room, he explained the situation. He told his staff about losing the sponsorship deal; he told them about Titan's bankruptcy; and he told them about Patrick's resignation.

His staff didn't seem upset. Jenny Ross, the marketing analyst, was the first to speak. "Honestly, we could really use that $5 million for something else. I've never understood why we'd give it to Walt Bigshot."

"It's Bigman," Mike Reed, the marketing manager, replied. "And of course Titan declared bankruptcy. No one ever shops there. I drive by their store every day, and I never see any cars in the parking lot. I'm surprised they lasted this long."

Then, the director of sports sponsorships, Barbara Gaines, chimed in. "And good riddance to Patrick. I know I shouldn't bash my boss, but since he's not my boss anymore, I guess he's fair game. He was a jerk . . . thought he knew everything. *Do this. Do that.* Maybe, now I can do some real marketing instead of doing Patrick's busy work."

This was unexpected. Everyone was taking the news rather well. Jim was expecting to spend the entire meeting doing damage control, but his staff seemed happier than ever.

"Well," Jim said with relief, "let's figure out what to do now. We have two problems I'd like us to address. First, our products aren't as relevant as they used to be, and second, we're not selling them where people like to shop. So?" Jim paused, then added, "What should we do?"

His staff responded with silence and blank looks on their faces.

"Come on, guys. Let's hear some ideas." Jim grabbed a marker, walked over to a flip cart, and stood there looking around the room. After a few awkward seconds, Jim said "Doesn't anyone have any ideas? Now's your chance."

Finally, Jenny spoke up. "You're asking us? I thought you'd tell us what to do."

"No. I'm interested in hearing your ideas. What do you think?"

One by one, his staff members started tossing out ideas for making their products more relevant. For over an hour, Jim stood at the flip chart and filled page after page with ideas. When one page filled up, he'd tear it off, tape it to the wall, and start writing on the next.

Some of the ideas were as simple as doing more television advertising. Others included paying for people to hold giant signs outside sporting goods stores and hiring a pilot to trail a giant *Premier Sports* banner behind an airplane. Mike even suggested they create their own radio talk show.

When the group finally stopped talking, Jim noticed that one of his staff members hadn't said a word. Lisa Brimmer, his insights manager, had been silent the entire meeting. Jim was afraid Lisa might have nothing to say, but he felt obligated to give her a chance. "Lisa, what do you think?"

She paused, then said softly, "Well, I've been thinking, before we start coming up with answers, shouldn't we ask a few questions first?"

"What do you mean?" Jim asked.

"I mean, how could we know what'll work if we don't know the *what, who, why,* and *where* of the situation?"

Jim's heart sank. He realized that Lisa might not have any idea what was going on. Had she really been sitting through the entire meeting without generating a single idea? And what was this about *what, who, why,* and *where*? He decided to give her one last chance. "Go on," he told Lisa.

"While everyone was talking, I wrote down four questions. I think we should answer these before deciding what we should do." She looked down at her notebook and cleared her throat. "First, what products should we focus on?"

As she read her list, Jim jotted the questions on the flipchart.

1. *What* products should we focus on?
2. *Who* makes the purchasing decisions for those products?
3. *Why* would people choose those products over others?
4. *Where* do they buy those products?

Lisa continued, "If we can answer these questions, we might come up with better ideas."

Barbara was the first to respond. "The *what* is easy. We sell football, baseball, and golf equipment. The *who* is also easy. Dads typically buy those products for their sons. As for the *why*, it's because their sports heroes endorse those products. And *where* is easy, too. They go to stores. With Titan Supercenters out of business, they'll have to go to other stores to buy our products."

Lisa didn't respond. After a brief silence, Jim said, "Lisa, tell us what you're thinking."

"Well, I'm not sure we have the right *what, who, why,* and *where*. I mean, if we keep doing the same things, why would anything change?" She looked down at her notebook. "Shouldn't we consider other sports?"

Jim thought about it for a second, and then said, "I think Lisa might be onto something. Since we're out of time for today, I want everyone to come back tomorrow with some ideas about the *what*. Specifically, tell me what other sports you think we should consider."

As everyone shuffled out of the conference room, Jim asked Lisa to stay behind.

"Lisa, why didn't you speak up earlier?"

"I don't know. It just never seemed like the right time."

"Well, we really need your help on this one. You're our insights person, and I have a feeling we'll need some new insights if we're gonna get through this."

"Okay." Lisa looked away. "May I go now?"

"Of course, but I'd like you to come back with some ideas for new products."

As Lisa walked out, Jim was left wondering whether she was really onto something.

***

That evening, Jim helped Sarah clean up after dinner. He told her all about his staff meeting and how odd Lisa's behavior seemed.

"You're such a guy," Sarah said.

He looked up from the dish he was drying. "What's that supposed to mean?"

"Guys tend to listen to the loudest person in the room. He who speaks loudest gets the most attention."

Jim felt annoyed by that comment. What did she want him to do? "Well, that's because people who speak up tend to have the most to say."

"Sometimes, the quiet ones have the most to say. But everyone is so busy listening to the loudmouths that they never hear the quiet ones."

For about an hour, Jim and Sarah discussed the differences between people who are outspoken and people who are quieter. Eventually, Jim admitted that Sarah had a good point. He made a mental note to keep encouraging all of his team members to contribute their ideas, especially the quieter ones.

Just then, Isabel, their ten-year-old daughter, danced into the kitchen.

Jim smiled at her quirkiness. "Hey Izzy, how's dance camp going?"

"Good. I'm getting really good with my pirouettes, and my teacher says I'm ready for pointe shoes!"

"That's great," Jim said with another smile.

"Not really," Sarah said. "That's just one more piece of sports gear we have to buy."

"Hey! You say that like there's something wrong with sports gear."

"Well, if your company'd sell dance shoes, maybe we could get a discount." Sarah turned to Isabel. "Okay. Off to bed."

2. What Products Should We Focus On?

The next day, Jim gathered his marketing team in the conference room, and he opened the discussion with, "Let's hear your ideas. What products should we focus on?"

Jenny started with *softball gear*. The others chimed in with *lacrosse, volleyball, soccer, martial arts,* and *laser tag*. Jim added *hoverboards* and *dance gear* to the list.

"Now, we need to prioritize these sports," Jim said. "How do we do that?"

To his surprise, Lisa raised her hand. "Yes, Lisa?" Jim asked.

"It should be simple algebra. You take the number of people who play each sport, multiply that by the average cost of gear per person, and multiply that by the market share we think we can get."

"Yeah, simple algebra," Mike nodded his head.

Jenny looked at him. "Have you even taken an algebra class?"

Mike admitted, "I'm not even sure how to spell algebra. Fortunately, I didn't need it since I majored in partying."

"Alright, guys," Jim said. "Let's split up into two teams and take a stab at the math. Each team will do research and make assumptions about each sport. Then, let's reconvene on Monday and compare results."

***

That evening, Jim asked his son, "How was your day?"

"Great!" Jake answered. "At taekwondo, I finally beat Dorian in sparring. It was close, but I won 6 to 5."

"Nice job. Tomorrow, I'd like to ask you some questions about taekwondo. I've got a project at work, and I could use your help."

"Sounds good. Maybe we can talk when you take me to my tournament."

"What tournament?"

"Oh, I forgot to tell you," Sarah said. "I need you to take Jake in the morning. His tournament's at the big arena on Beacon Street, and you'll need to be there by eight o'clock."

"Eight o'clock on a Saturday? You're kidding me," Jim said.

"Well, you better get the kids off to bed." Sarah couldn't contain a grin. "You gotta get up early tomorrow."

***

The next morning, Jim called for Jake to meet him in the driveway. When Jake got into the car, he was carrying the biggest duffle bag Jim had ever seen.

"What's in the bag?" Jim asked with an eyebrow raised.

"My new sparring gear. Now that I'm a green belt, I get to spar."

"Must be a lot of gear," Jim said.

When Jim parked at the arena, he noticed several dozen kids walking across the parking lot, all carrying similar duffle bags. As Jim walked into the giant arena, he saw several hundred more kids, all with big duffle bags.

"Jake?" Jim said as he looked around. "How much did your sparring gear cost?"

"About $300. I thought Mom'd freak when Master Chan told her the price, but she was fine with it. She figured you wouldn't mind now that you're making the big bucks."

Jim quickly did the math: $300 for gear times roughly 400 kids at the tournament equaled over $100,000. He wondered how many kids were doing martial arts across the country and how many were paying $300 for their gear.

***

When Jim's team reconvened on Monday, Barbara started. "We came up with martial arts as the best option. The other sports either didn't have enough people participating, the cost of gear was too low, or we didn't think we could get enough market share to build a big enough business."

"How did you figure out how many people play each sport?" Jim asked.

"We just did some simple online searches."

Mike reported for the other team. "We also came up with martial arts, so great minds think alike."

After discussing the numbers, Jim said, "Okay, let's go with martial arts. Lisa, what's the next question?"

Lisa looked at her notebook. "The next question is *who makes the purchase decisions for those products?* We should find some people involved with martial arts and find out who decides which brands to buy."

"Sounds good," Jim responded. "I have a son who does taekwondo, so I'll check with him."

Barbara chimed in, "My niece does karate, so I'll check with her."

Jenny and Mike also knew people who were involved with martial arts, so they offered to do research too.

"Great," Jim said. "Let's find out who makes the purchase decisions and report back on Wednesday."

As the group disbanded, Jim felt invigorated by his team's enthusiasm, but he was unsure about the approach they were taking on this project. It seemed backwards to have his staff members defining the process and being involved in such strategic decisions. Typically, company leaders make the big decisions, and the staff just executes the plans. Hopefully, their unconventional approach would work.

Jim went to the break room, where he saw Olivia Whitten. "Olivia, how are things going in operations?" Jim asked.

"Okay," she responded. "I'm going on a trip to China next week to meet with some of our suppliers."

"Ah, cool. Hey, do you know if any of them make martial arts equipment?"

"I don't know, but I can find out. Why do you ask?"

Just then, Barbara walked into the break room. "Jim, can I talk with you about the karate gear we're working on?"

"Karate gear?" Olivia asked. "I didn't know we're working on karate gear."

Jim responded, "If you have a minute, we can tell you about our idea." Jim invited Olivia and Barbara to join him in his office. They spent the next twenty minutes talking about their idea for a new line of martial arts gear.

"I love it!" Olivia exclaimed. "If we can convince Ed to support this, we might actually launch something new for a change."

"What about Francis and Sam?" Jim asked.

"Let me handle them," Olivia replied. "You just figure out what we need, and I'll take care of Frank and Sammy."

3. Who Makes the Purchase Decisions?

That night, Jim and Sarah were talking after their kids went to bed. "How are things going at work?" Sarah asked.

"Good," Jim replied. "My team's working on turning our business around."

"Great! Do they have any good ideas?"

"I think so. We're looking into other sports to see if we can expand our product line. Right now, we're thinking about martial arts gear."

"Well, my vote is *yes*. We spent a fortune on Jake's sparring gear."

"Hey, maybe you could help me with that. Can you ask some of the dads how they picked the brand of gear they bought for their kids?"

"Ha! That's a joke!" Sarah glared at Jim. "Dads don't buy stuff for kids. Moms do. Or, these days, kids buy stuff for themselves."

"Since when?" Jim asked.

"Well, when was the last time you bought something for our kids?"

"I bought Jake's birthday present."

"Nope. That was me."

"Okay. How 'bout his Christmas present?"

"Try again. I gave him a gift card, and he bought his own presents."

"So, we probably shouldn't ask dads what they want when they're looking for gear."

"Nope. You should ask moms. Or better yet, just ask the kids." Sarah paused and added, "For Jake's sparring gear, I just gave him a gift card and he bought it himself."

Jim nodded. "Guess I could ask him."

Jim went upstairs and knocked on Jake's bedroom door. He heard, "Come in," so he went inside.

"S'up dad," he heard as he entered the bedroom.

"Hey Jake," Jim said softly. "Can I ask you a question?"

"You just did," Jake responded with a snicker. "Now, if you must, ask me another."

Jim smirked, then asked Jake how he decided which brand of sparring gear to buy.

"Master Chan told me," Jake replied. "He tells everyone which gear to buy."

"So, you didn't pick the brand yourself?"

"No. I wouldn't know one brand from another."

Jim thought about this. Maybe he should have a conversation with Master Chan.

***

The next evening, Jim went with Jake to his taekwondo class. After the class, he asked Master Chan about the gear.

"We tell everyone to get gear from the Kickalot brand," Master Chan said.

"Do you know if other instructors pick the brands, or do they have the students choose?"

"The instructors always choose. We need to be the experts since the kids don't know anything about the brands."

Jim thanked Master Chan and went home with Jake.

***

The next morning, Jim met with Barbara and Lisa. Barbara confirmed that her niece's karate instructor picked the brand of gear that the kids used. Barbara's sister paid for the gear, but the instructor told her which brand to buy.

Jim called Jenny and Mike into his office. "So, what did you learn?" he asked. They reported the same thing. The instructors were the primary decision makers.

Jim asked, "Did anyone say that dads were involved in buying the gear?"

Everyone replied, "No." According to their research, dads had nothing to do with the purchase decisions.

Jenny looked at Jim, then the others. "So, we've been approaching this all wrong. How could we miss something so obvious?"

"It's called *confirmation bias*," Lisa said. "We've been looking for things to confirm our own beliefs, not things that are true. We wanted to believe dads make all the decisions because we're good at marketing to dads."

"Oh." Mike looked at Lisa with relief. "I thought it might be because we're idiots."

Jenny turned to Mike. "I'm going with confirmation bias for me. You, on the other hand . . ." Mike frowned as everyone else chuckled.

"This is a huge deal," Jim said. "Now that we know who makes the decisions, this will completely change our approach. Let's hold off on any more athlete deals and start doing research on instructors."

4. Why Would People Choose Those Products?

Jim turned to Lisa. "So, what's next?"

Lisa looked back at her notebook. "Why would people choose those products over others?"

"Okay. Everyone talk with some instructors and find out what they want from their martial arts gear," Jim instructed.

***

On Saturday afternoon, Jim went with Jake to his taekwondo class. When they walked into the gym, Master Chan said, "Hey, Mr. Harrison. Welcome back. Why don't you suit up and join the class?"

Jim laughed and gave Jake a wink. "No thanks. I'm not interested in giving Jake a chance to beat me up."

Jim watched the class intently. He noticed kids putting on their sparring gear, which took the first few minutes of the class. Then, he watched them spar. He noticed that many of the kids had to pause to adjust their pads and reattach straps that had come undone.

After the class, Jim asked Master Chan if they could talk about the sparring gear. "Sure," Master Chan replied. "Can we meet up this evening?"

"I think so. I'll call Sarah to see what our plans are for dinner. Maybe you could join us?"

"Yeah, sounds great. My wife and daughter are at a mother-daughter camp this weekend. Eating with you sounds better than fending for myself."

Jim called Sarah, and she confirmed that she was fine with hosting a dinner guest.

***

When Master Chan arrived at their home, Jim invited him into the family room.

"Thanks for coming over," Jim said. "I have some questions about the gear your students use." He explained that he worked at a sporting goods company, and they were thinking about launching a new line of martial arts gear.

"That's great," Master Chan said. "If you name it after me, I'll give you all the advice you want."

Jim chuckled. They spent a few minutes talking about the sporting goods business, then Sarah walked into the room and said, "That's enough work for now. Let's eat."

After dinner, Jim and Master Chan went back into the family room and continued their conversation.

"So, how'd you become a taekwondo instructor?" Jim asked.

"Taekwondo was an important part of my childhood," Master Chan explained. "When I was a boy, I was a little stinker before I started doing martial arts. It taught me discipline and focus, and I want to pass that on to future generations."

"Is that why you started your own business?"

"Yes, I wanted to help people improve themselves, and I wanted to give them a good experience with taekwondo. That way, they'll want to keep doing it. And, I want them to tell their friends so I get more people to train. I'd like everything in my gym to be a positive experience."

"Does that influence the brand of equipment you choose?"

Master Chan paused and said, "I never really thought about it that way. The equipment is just a tool, you know? Like your hands are a tool. Tools serve a purpose. I teach people to focus their energy. If the equipment helps them focus, it's doing its job."

"Is your equipment helping people focus?"

"When it's comfortable, yes. That's why I switched from the brand we used to use. The kids were constantly complaining about the old gear being uncomfortable, so they weren't focusing on their lessons."

"I noticed that the sparring gear takes a long time to put on. Is that a problem?"

"I guess it is. Students spend the first few minutes of every class getting into their gear." He thought a moment. "Yeah, it takes a while to get geared up. I guess that time could be used better."

"And the straps seem to pop loose. Is that a problem?"

"Oh yeah, for sure. Every time a student needs to stop and re-strap their gear, it disrupts their focus. Plus, while they're sparring, they might be concerned that their straps'll come undone." He shook his head smiling. "Man, if you could solve that, they'd be a lot less distracted and a lot more focused on what they're doing."

"Is there anything else that can be improved?" Jim asked.

"Nothing comes to mind. I'll think about it, and I'll let you know. Now, I really must go." Master Chan stood up. "It's getting late. Thanks for the hospitality, and please tell your wife that I enjoyed the wonderful dinner."

Sarah walked into the room. "You can tell her yourself. It's been a pleasure having you here, and I do apologize for Jim conducting research on you."

"Oh no, it's been my pleasure," Master Chan said. "If he can find a way to help my students, he can conduct whatever research he wants on me."

As they said goodnight, Jim thought about changing Premier's approach to marketing. Rather than focusing on famous athletes, maybe he should focus on helping instructors accomplish their goals. He wondered how his new line of sporting gear could do that.

***

On Monday, Jim met with the rest of his staff. They explained how they found similar issues during their interviews with other martial arts instructors. They agreed to capture the opportunities and send their notes to Jim in emails.

"Please copy Olivia on those emails," Jim said. "She's a part of our team now, and I want her to help us find the new equipment we'll need."

5. Where Do They Buy Those Products?

Jim turned to Lisa and asked, "What's our next question?"

She flipped through her notebook, found the page she was looking for. "Where do they buy those products?"

"Okay, everyone," Jim said. "You know the drill. Go find out where people buy their martial arts gear. We'll regroup on Wednesday."

***

That evening, Jim was talking to Jake about his taekwondo gear. "Where'd you buy your gear?"

"Kickalot.com," Jake replied.

Jim pulled up the website, and he was impressed by what he saw. With very little effort, he was able to find a wide variety of gear available for purchase on the site.

Next, Jim pulled up the Premier Sporting Goods website so he could compare the sites side-by-side. The Premier site only had information about the company's history and its executives.

There was no information about the products, and there was no way to purchase anything from the site.

Jim's stomach sank as he realized how far behind Premier was compared to other companies. He knew other sporting goods suppliers were starting to sell their products online, but he didn't realize how good their e-commerce sites were.

Jim spent the next few hours researching other company websites. He saw a wide range from sites that were as limited as Premier's to sites that we're even better than Kickalot's.

He picked up the phone, called Master Chan, and asked him what percent of the sparring gear was purchased online.

"Nearly all of it," Master Chan responded. "A few people order from the catalog in my office, but almost everyone goes straight to the website."

"Does anyone go to a store to buy their gear?"

"No. I don't think Kickalot even sells gear in stores."

Jim thanked Master Chan, said good-bye. As he hung up the phone, Jim sat back and thought about how outdated Premier's approach had become. It was no wonder their top retailers were in trouble. Since people weren't going to stores to buy sporting equipment, Premier would have to shift focus quickly from brick-and-mortar stores to e-commerce sites.

6. There's Gonna Be a Shoot-out!

The next day, Ed Baxter called Jim and Sam into his office. "I'd like an update on your plans to turn our business around." Ed turned to Sam. "You first."

Sam suggested the company host a big golf tournament for the leaders of MegaSports Incorporated and Behemoth Athletic

Supply. "Now that Titan is going out of business," Sam explained, "sales will shift to MegaSports and Behemoth. We need to work harder than ever to build relationships with their executives."

"Okay." Ed turned to Jim. "And you?"

Jim explained what his team had learned about the martial arts opportunity. He suggested that Premier quickly expand their product line to include martial arts gear and start marketing it directly to instructors.

"Nah, it's way too risky." Sam said dismissively. "It'd take us years to develop a new product line, and we don't know anything about selling products online. Plus, it would kill our relationships with our top retailers. I'm not approving anything that would jeopardize our relationships with them."

Ed responded, "I'd like to hear more about both ideas. I want both of you to prepare presentations that show how your idea will help our business. Then, let's have our investment bankers choose how we spend our $5 million."

"All right!" Sam said. "There's gonna be a shoot-out!"

"Sounds good to me," Jim said. "I'll get my team started on our martial arts proposal."

Sam and Jim agreed to present their business proposals to the investment bankers during the quarterly investment meeting that was a few months away. The winner would get the $5 million to execute his business plan.

Step 3: Define the Current Customer Journey

1. Start with the Customer Journey

As Jim and Sarah relaxed in their family room, Sarah asked how the project was coming along.

"Great. I'm really excited about it," Jim replied. "We've got some good ideas for our new line of martial arts gear. The only problem is finding out how to sell it."

"What do you mean?" Sarah asked.

"In the past, our company's focus has been on getting displays in sporting goods stores. The problem is that most purchases are now made online. We don't sell anything online, so we're not sure where to start."

Sarah thought about it for a minute, then blurted out, "Hey, isn't your friend Ethan at a digital marketing agency? Why don't you call him?"

Jim shook his head. Why didn't he think of that? He kissed his clever wife and picked up the phone to call Ethan.

"Yo, Jim! What's up?" Ethan answered.

"Ethan, I could use your help. I need some marketing advice."

"Yeah? Well, it's gonna cost you. Now that you're a CMO, my rates are going up."

"Ha, ha. Okay, I'll pay you double what I paid last time you gave me marketing advice."

"Sure. Let me do the math. Last time, you paid me . . . let's see. If I remember right . . . you paid me . . . nothing. Now, according to my calculations, if I take nothing and double it . . . hmmm . . . that's a tough one. I think it's . . . nothing."

"Yeah, and your advice will probably be worth exactly that."

"Ha, ha. I don't have all night, so tell me what's going on."

Jim explained the situation at his company. He told Ethan that he needed to come up with a plan to turn the business around. Otherwise, Premier Sporting Goods would likely go bankrupt, and Jim would lose his job

"Well, we better get to work," Ethan replied. "I'm leaving town tomorrow morning for one of Sophie's soccer tournaments, and I won't be back until late Sunday night. How 'bout we talk next week?"

"I was hoping to get started sooner. Do you have any time to talk this weekend?"

"No way, man! We have games all day tomorrow and Sunday, and I won't get home until late Sunday night."

"Come on," Jim said. "You gotta give me somethin'. I've got all weekend to think about this, and I've got nothing."

"How's this? Think back to what Professor Anderson said when we were in business school. Where should you always start?"

Jim thought for a moment, then responded, "Start with the customer journey."

"Winner, winner, chicken dinner!" Ethan shouted. "Now, get to work. Call me next week. Gotta go."

"Thanks man. Have a good weekend," Jim said as he hung up the phone.

Jim hadn't noticed that Sarah had left the house. He found a note on the kitchen island that said, "Went to store. Be back soon."

Jim grabbed a beer from the refrigerator, popped it open, and started thinking about Ethan's advice. As he took a sip, he walked into his den and found his marketing notebook from business school. He flipped through the pages until he found the one titled *Customer Journey*.

On that page, Jim saw the following notes:

Customer Journey:
- *outlines the steps a shopper takes to decide what to purchase*
- *you can influence the shopper to choose your brand by understanding these steps*

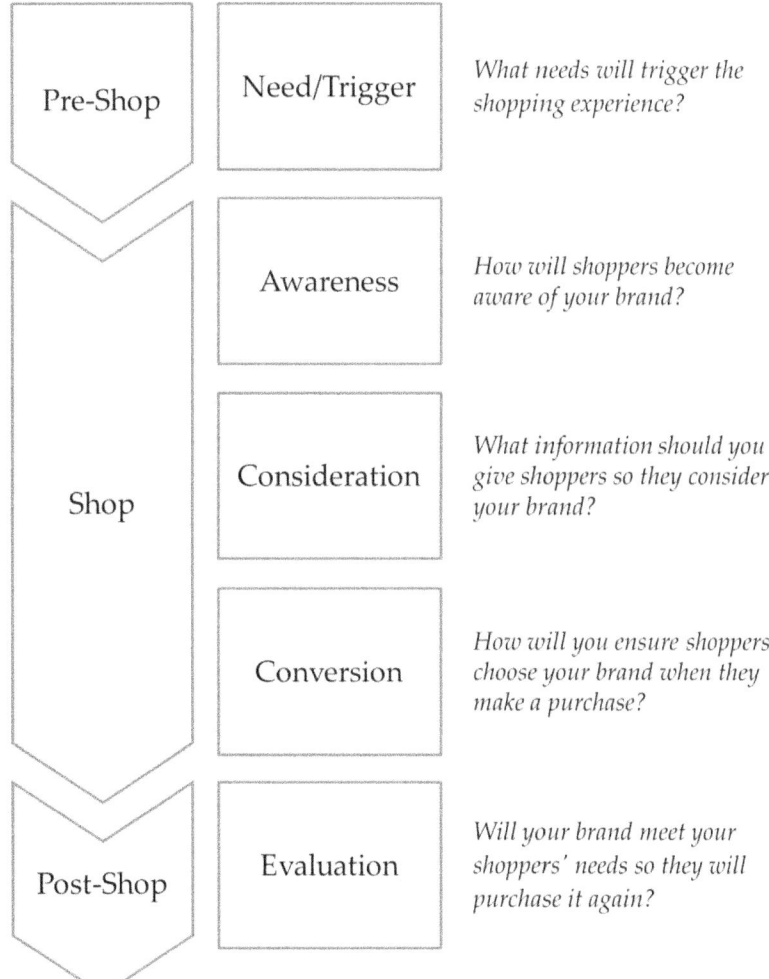

Jim took out his digital tablet, opened his note-taking app, and entered the following:

1. Pre-Shop: What triggers the purchase?

2. Shop:
   A. Awareness: How do customers become aware of new brands?
   B. Consideration: Where do they get information about brands?
   C. Purchase: How is the actual purchase made?

3. Post-Shop: What ensures a re-purchase?

Jim called Master Chan, explained that he had more questions, and asked if they could get together for another discussion. "Can I buy you a beer in exchange for your time?"

"Sure," responded Master Chan. "How's tomorrow afternoon? I could meet you at Joe's Cafe around 5:00?"

Jim agreed, thanked Master Chan, and said goodbye.

2. What Triggers a Purchase?

The next day, Jim explained the Customer Journey to Master Chan, who agreed to tell Jim everything he could about the process for buying martial arts gear. "I'd like to understand how you choose your equipment so I can figure out what triggers a purchase," Jim said.

Master Chan explained that he used IronStrike sparring gear for years. It was more durable than other brands, so he felt like he was helping his students save money with gear that lasted longer.

A few years ago, IronStrike announced that they had improved their gear to make it nearly indestructible. With their new design, they guaranteed the gear would last at least two years or they'd provide a full refund.

Master Chan noticed that students started complaining that the new gear was uncomfortable. They would spar for a few minutes, then they would ask to take the gear off.

"I couldn't keep the students focused," explained Master Chan. "They were distracted by their uncomfortable pads and helmets. We just weren't accomplishing anything during the sparring sessions."

"So, can you describe what's most important when you pick out sparring gear?" Jim asked.

"Okay. The gear needs to protect students from hits and kicks during sparring. It needs to be strong enough to absorb contact but soft enough to feel comfortable while they're wearing it."

"What emotional benefits should the gear provide?" Jim asked.

"Emotional benefits? Hmm. Never thought of that." Master Chan paused. "Well, I guess it helps students feel confident. When gear's working properly, they can focus on building their skills. As they get better at their technique, they feel better about themselves. That helps 'em get stronger and feel more independent. You know?"

"Okay, so let me make sure I got this right. Sparring gear needs to have two main functional benefits: it needs to be strong enough to protect students and flexible enough to be comfortable. The emotional benefits include focus and confidence, which means students can become stronger and more independent. Does that sound right?"

"It sounds like a lot for sparring gear to do, but yeah, it's right."

Jim added the following notes on his digital tablet.

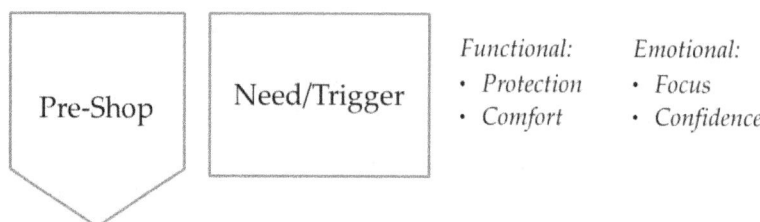

3. How Do You Learn About New Brands?

Next, Jim asked, "So, how did you learn about new brands?"

Master Chan explained that he started hearing about Kickalot several years ago. "I first noticed them at tournaments where I saw their banners and t-shirts. Then, I saw their ads on martial arts websites. Some sites even featured articles about their gear."

"Can you think of other places where you might notice new martial arts brands?" Jim asked.

"Well, when I'm on YouTube watching videos about coaching techniques, I've noticed ads for a new brand of breakable boards," Master Chan said. "They've got these great video ads that show people breaking boards in slow motion. The ads are simple, but they really catch my eye."

"Great. Is there anywhere else we should consider when we advertise a new brand?"

Master Chan mentioned an online store where he purchases his belts, certificates, and trophies. "I like that site because it has ideas for rewarding my students. Plus, they've got ratings and reviews for the products they sell," Master Chan explained.

"Okay, let's see if I've got this right," Jim said. "Some of the places you see new brands are banners and t-shirts at tournaments, ads and articles on martial arts websites, and short video ads on YouTube. You also mentioned online stores where you buy supplies. Anywhere else?"

"That's all I can think of," Master Chan said. "I'll tell you if I think of anything else."

4. Where Do You Go to Get More Information?

Next, Jim asked "Where do you go to get more information about a brand?"

Master Chan explained that he went to online discussion groups to ask other instructors about the brand. "Several of them said Kickalot's gear was very flexible, and students never complained about it feeling uncomfortable. This was credible 'cause it came directly from other instructors."

He also searched for reviews on video sites. "Several video bloggers posted reviews of Kickalot's gear, and they really liked it. I was especially impressed with the reviews that showed students using the gear. I tend to trust those more than ads, you know? Reviewers aren't as biased."

"Yeah, true." Jim said. "Did you find the brand in any online stores?"

Master Chan nodded. "Yes. The ratings were very high on those sites, and the reviews were generally positive. Several reviews mentioned that the gear had a good balance of strength and flexibility."

"How about Kickalot's website?" Jim asked.

"Well, actually, it was a bit disappointing," Master Chan said. They showed photos of their gear, but they didn't include much information. That's a place where they could definitely improve."

"Did you do any other research?"

"When I was at a tournament, I noticed a booth with a Kickalot banner. They had samples of their gear, so I could see it in person. I had a few of my students try it on and test it out. They said it was a lot more comfortable than the IronStrike gear."

"Okay, let me see if I've captured everything," Jim said. He added to his diagram and asked Master Chan to take a look.

"Yeah, that looks right," Master Chan responded.

Jim felt energized. He was starting to imagine how this information could lead to a great marketing campaign.

5. What Causes You to Purchase?

"I'm getting the hang of this," Master Chan said. "What's next?"

Jim smiled. "Now, let's talk about conversion. Specifically, what casuses you to purchase the new brand? Tell me how you went from considering the brand to actually buying it."

Master Chan described a conversation he had with a Kickalot representative at a tournament. "She offered me a complete set of sparring gear at half price. If I didn't like it, I could send it back for a full refund." He shrugged. "I took her up on it."

He described how the sales representative took his measurements and sent him gear that was his size. When the gear arrived, Master Chan was impressed with how well it fit. After using it for a few days, he decided to make the switch.

"I called the company and asked them how my students could place orders. They walked me through their online store, and I've been sending students there ever since."

"Could they have done anything to make the purchase process easier?"

"Uh… yeah, I think so. It wasn't easy to find their online store. I tried to search for it, but their site didn't show up on search engines. Plus, once I was on the site, the ordering process was a bit clumsy."

"Good. That means we can do something better." Jim updated his diagram to include the following information in the Shop section.

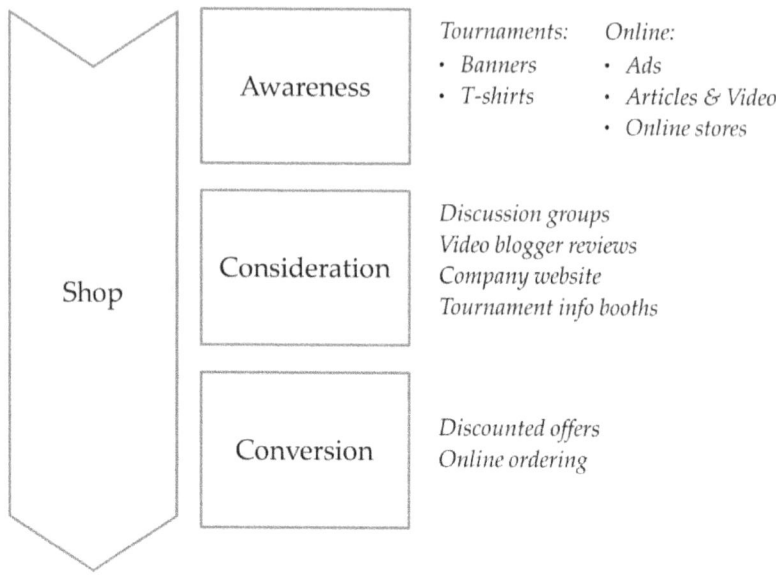

6. What Can Ensure a Re-Purchase?

Jim explained, "Next, I want to know what can ensure a re-purchase." He asked Master Chan about his experiences since he purchased the Kickalot gear.

"Yeah, it's been okay. The gear is more comfortable than IronStrike's, but it takes longer to put on. Plus, it has the issue with the straps that we talked about."

"How's their customer service?"

"Not very good. Their shipping lead-times are very inconsistent. Sometimes, their orders arrive in a few days. Sometimes, it takes weeks. Then, when I call them with an issue, it's almost impossible to speak to an actual person."

"That sounds like another area of opportunity."

"Yes," Master Chan agreed. "They could definitely do a better job after the sale."

Jim added the following information to his diagram:

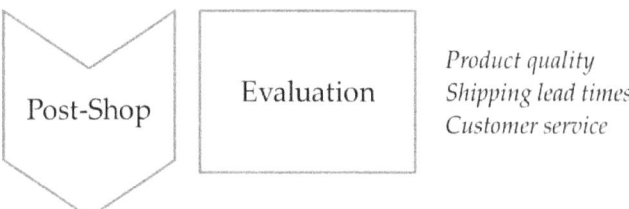

"Good. That should be enough for now. I can't tell you how much I appreciate your input." Jim paid the check and said goodnight.

Step 4: Design a Better Experience

1. What Should We Call Our Brand?

When Jim arrived at the office on Monday, Olivia pulled into the parking lot next to him. As they walked toward the building together, Jim asked, "How was your trip to China?"

"Very productive," Olivia replied. "You'll love what I have to tell you." She explained how one of their suppliers just launched a line of martial arts gear in Asia, and they were looking for a partner to help them launch it in the United States.

"Their gear is fantastic," Olivia explained. "It uses a new stretchy cloth material, so there are no straps to come undone. Plus, it's much quicker to put on, and it's very comfortable."

"Great!" Jim said. "Can you get some samples for us to try?"

"I'm way ahead of you," Olivia replied. "The samples already shipped, and they should be here later this week."

As Jim and Olivia entered the building, they passed Sam. "Howdy partner. High noon's a comin'. You ready to get filled with lead?"

"What?" Jim replied.

"Come on." Sam grinned. "The shoot-out's comin'. My presentation's going to blow you away. You and your team'll be headin' out of Dodge when the investment bankers get a load of my plans."

"Okay. I look forward to seeing your proposal," Jim said as he walked away. He couldn't stand the idea of losing to Sam. He just hoped his team could get their plan together before the meeting with the investment bankers.

Later that morning, Jim called his entire staff into the conference room. "Great news!" he told them. "Olivia found a new line of martial arts gear that's perfect for us. Now, we just need to develop our marketing plan."

"That's fantastic," Jenny replied. "Where do we start?"

Jim explained the Customer Journey model to them, and they agreed to meet for two hours every day that week to work on the details. They started that afternoon with the Pre-Shop stage.

Jim explained that Pre-Shop involved identifying the triggers that lead to a purchase. "We need to find out why martial arts instructors might be interested in switching brands. Here's what I learned over the weekend."

He described his conversation with Master Chan and how martial arts gear needs to protect students in a comfortable way.

"So, if Kickalot's gear already does that, what can we possibly offer?" Mike asked.

"The problem is that their pads don't consistently protect the students," Jim replied. "When the straps come loose, students have to stop what they're doing. Plus, it takes so long to put on their gear that students are losing precious training time. The pads that Olivia found in China should fix those problems."

"I see," Jenny said. "Now that we've identified the benefits we can provide, we just need to communicate those benefits to instructors."

Jim was happy to hear the enthusiasm in Jenny's voice. He was sensing a new energy in his team. It urged him on. "Now, let's work on our marketing message so we know exactly what we want to communicate."

They spent the rest of the afternoon discussing ways to communicate the benefits that their gear would provide.

"So, what should we call our brand?" Jim asked.

"How about Strong & Soft?" Mike said.

"That sounds like a brand of toilet paper." Jenny replied.

They all laughed. After several other failed attempts, Lisa finally chimed in. "How about *Chikara*?" she suggested.

"What does that mean?" Jenny asked.

"It's *strength* in Japanese," Lisa responded.

"Chikara sounds too much like chicken," Mike said. Again, the group burst out laughing.

"What's the Japanese word for focus?" Barbara asked.

Lisa typed something into her phone. Then, she replied, "*Fokasu.*"

"I like it," Jim said. "Let's run that name by some martial arts instructors and see what they think."

"I can prepare a survey for instructors," Lisa said, "and I'll include a question about the name *Fokasu*."

"Alright, sounds like a plan," Jim replied. "That's all for today. Tomorrow, we'll fokasu on how we generate awareness for our brand." He grinned, pleased with his wit. The group looked at him and let out a collective groan. "C'mon? No love for our new brand?"

"Oh, we love our new brand," Jenny responded. "It's just . . . well . . . how 'bout you stick to the leading, we'll cover the humor from now on."

As the group disbanded, chattering amongst themselves, Jim thought about the progress they had made. In a few weeks, they had gone from struggling to find direction to having a clear goal. He was pleased to see his team coming together and working on a unified objective.

***

That evening, Jim called Ethan.

"Whazup?" Ethan said when he answered the phone.

"I'm making good progress on the Customer Journey." Jim told Ethan about his conversation with Master Chan.

"That's great," Ethan said. "Now, all you have to do is create a better Customer Journey."

"Any advice?"

"When I work on Customer Journeys with my clients, I remind them to concentrate on three things. First, make sure you have an extremely compelling message. Second, get awareness for your brand by communicating that message using media where your target audience is most receptive. And third, make sure all roads lead to a purchase."

"Got it," Jim replied. He thanked Ethan and hung up.

2. Use a "Get, To, By, Because" Framework

The next day, Jim told his team, "I've asked our attorney to see if the Fokasu brand name is available. Assuming so, we'll need to build awareness for it. Let's spend today aligning on a campaign brief and brainstorming ideas for our ads." He motioned to the woman sitting next to him. "I invited Cindy Carter from our creative agency to join us. You all know Cindy, so let's get started."

To define their campaign goals, the team decided to use a *Get, To, By, Because* framework. With Cindy's help, they wrote the following objectives:

GET: martial arts instructors
TO: tell their students to buy Fokasu sparring gear
BY: showing them that Fokasu can help their students focus on their lessons
BECAUSE: Fokasu delivers the perfect blend of strength, comfort, and consistency

The team generated several dozen ideas for marketing messages. They prioritized their top choices, then agreed to survey martial arts instructors to get their input. Next, they worked on identifying places to advertise their new brand. Their top ideas included tournaments, video sites, martial arts blogs, online stores, and search engines.

Lisa agreed to include questions about the media choices in the short survey she was preparing for martial arts instructors. Cindy took the creative brief back to her agency team to start generating advertising concepts.

Jim was pleased with his team. They were making good progress thanks to the insights they identified together. He just hoped it would be enough with the shootout only a few months away.

3. We Should Have Debates Like This

The next day was more challenging. Jim started the work session by explaining the Consideration stage of the journey. "Once we have awareness for our brand," he said, "we need to give instructors enough information that they'll consider purchasing our products. What are some ways we can communicate that information?"

The team members listed ideas including video reviews, a brand website, and sales people to call on martial arts instructors.

The team frequently disagreed about which tools would be most effective. After one particularly heated discussion, Jenny turned to Jim and said, "We can't seem to agree on anything today. What's wrong with us?"

Jim responded, "Nothing. We should have debates like this. Rigorous debating is a good way for us to evaluate ideas. We all need to feel comfortable expressing our points of view, even if others disagree. Then, we can make informed decisions after everyone's weighed in."

"It just doesn't feel like we're making progress," Jenny said.

"Actually, we're making a lot of progress," Lisa replied. "Let me draw the Customer Journey that we've defined so far. Once you see it on the whiteboard, I think you'll feel better."

Jim was pleased to see Lisa speaking out. She seemed to have a unique ability to listen for extended periods of time and organize information in clear, meaningful ways.

"Okay Lisa, let's see it," Jim said.

She went to the whiteboard and started drawing. "It seems like we're building a big funnel," she explained. "At the opening, we're trying to pull instructors into the funnel with messages that get their attention. Then, we pull them in further with content that's relevant for them. Finally, we direct them to a specific place where they'll purchase our products."

When she was finished drawing, this diagram was on the whiteboard.

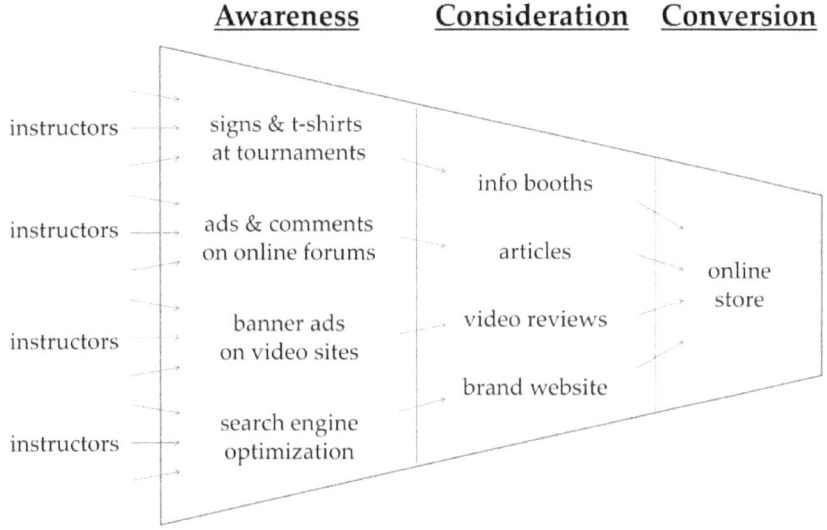

"That's exactly right. That's exactly what we need to do." Jim sat back in his chair with a smile. He was thrilled that Lisa captured the shopping process in such a clear way. The rest of the group nodded and smiled.

"Jim, I have a question," Jenny said. "Why didn't you tell us about this funnel thing earlier?" she asked with a grin.

"Actually, I didn't think of it." Jim turned to Lisa and said, "Good job."

Just then, there was a knock on the door. Olivia peeked into the room. "May I interrupt?"

"Of course," Jim replied. "Come on in."

Olivia walked into the room pulling a cart behind her. On the cart were several boxes. "Anyone want to see a surprise from China?"

Jim's eyes lit up. "Are those the samples?"

"Yes," Olivia replied. "I have several sets of sparring gear from our supplier, plus samples from IronStrike and Kickalot. Let's check 'em out."

The team dug into the boxes and started putting on the gear. They instantly noticed that the IronStrike gear was rigid and uncomfortable. The Kickalot gear was more flexible, but with all the straps, it took much longer to put on. The new equipment from China had the best balance of protection and comfort. Plus, it was easy to put on, and it stayed in place without issues.

"We have a winner!" Mike was raising his hands in the air. "Now, we just need a good marketing team to market this stuff." He looked around the room. "Oh, wait. We're the marketing team. Well, we better get to work."

Jim smiled. "Olivia, thanks for finding this gear. It's perfect." He let the team play a bit longer, then said, "That's it for today. Tomorrow, we'll continue with the Conversion section of the Customer Journey. See you then."

As Jim walked out of the conference room, he was overflowing with excitement. He was so proud of his team and grateful to have Oliva on his side.

4. Get Reactions from our Target Audience

The next day, as the team gathered in the conference room, Sam Baxter opened the door and said, "Bang! Bang!"

Jenny jumped out of her chair and turned to Sam with a scowl on her face. "What?"

"Bang! Bang!" repeated Sam. "High noon's comin', and y'all should be running for the hills."

"Very funny," Jim replied. "You may be taking this shootout thing a little too seriously."

Sam chuckled and closed the door.

"That's it," Lisa said. "Now I'm mad. Let's get to work."

The other team members looked at each other and burst out laughing. They began their meeting with renewed determination.

The group had an intense debate about how they should sell their gear. "As I see it, we have three options," Jim explained. "We can sell it in brick-and-mortar stores where we currently sell our products; we can sell it in existing online stores; or we can sell it directly to consumers in an online store that we build ourselves."

Barbara argued for selling it in stores where they currently sold their products. "We already have the infrastructure and the relationships with those retailers," she explained. "Why should we create something new when we've invested so much in our current system?"

Mike made the case for existing online stores. "They already have a base of customer traffic," he argued. "Plus, we could start by using their infrastructure, and then we could build our own e-commerce site later."

Jenny took the side of creating their own online store. "If we sell our products using our own site, we won't have to pay fees to other retailers. We'll make more money by selling directly to consumers."

After a lengthy debate, Jim turned to Lisa and asked, "What do you think?"

In a calm, logical voice, Lisa said, "Sorry, Barbara. Your argument is based on sunk costs. It doesn't matter how much we've invested in the past. The only things that matter are future revenues and future costs. Since our target customers aren't buying gear at brick-and-mortar stores, it's not likely we'll get much future revenue from that option."

Lisa looked at Jenny and said, "Jenny, in the long run, I like your idea. It could be the most profitable option, but it'll take time for us to build the infrastructure and the traffic for our own e-commerce site. I recommend we build that option later, but we don't lead with it."

Lisa turned to Jim and said, "I'm voting for Mike's idea. It's the quickest to implement, and it's likely to generate the most income."

"Booyah!" Mike threw his hands in the air. "Who's the man? This guy!" he said as he pointed to himself.

The others looked at him and grimaced. Jim said, "As much as I hate to say it, I agree. All in favor?" Barbara and Lisa reluctantly nodded. "Okay, let's start researching sites that can sell our new gear. Tomorrow, we'll meet and review advertising concepts from our agency."

Lisa said, "I'll also have a draft of our instructors' survey for us to review. I'd like to send it out quickly so we can get reactions from our target audience."

5. Let's See Some Advertising Ideas

On Friday morning, Jim started the meeting by saying, "I have three topics for today. First, we'll briefly cover the final stage of the Customer Journey. Second, we'll review the initial advertising concepts from our agency. And, third, we'll review Lisa's draft of the instructors' survey. Anything else?"

"Nope," Jenny said. "Let's get started."

The group discussed ways to follow up with customers. They agreed to send emails to customers thanking them for their purchases. They would also offer instructors free pamphlets to give to their students. Those pamphlets would have simple, clear instructions for buying the sparring gear online.

"Before we see the advertising concepts," Jim announced, "I have some good news. Our attorney confirmed that the Fokasu name is available if we want to use it for our brand." The team agreed to move forward with that name. "Great!" Jim said. "Now, let's see some advertising ideas."

As the group reviewed the concepts, they selected an option that blended the functional benefits of the Fokasu gear with the emotional benefits that it provided.

Then, they reviewed the survey that Lisa prepared. They agreed to include questions about the brand name, the marketing messages, the media options, and pricing. "Perfect," Lisa said after the group had given their feedback. "I'll incorporate your input and send out the survey this afternoon. I should have results early next week."

Jim thanked his team for a very productive week. "On Monday, we'll start building the actual Customer Experience, and we'll start working on our presentation for the executive team."

"Finally," Jenny said. "It's about time we start taking shots at the Baxter brothers."

"The Baxter brothers!" Mike said. "I like that. It sounds like a gang of outlaws."

The group let out a collective "Ugh," and adjourned for the week.

6. Stop Talking and Start Doing

That evening, Jim called Ethan again.

"Come on, Jim," Ethan said when he answered the phone. "If you keep calling me, I'm going to have to start charging you."

"Yeah, yeah," Jim responded. "Now, shut up and listen." Jim explained the progress his team had made. When he was done, he asked, "Any advice on next steps?"

There was no response. "Ethan, are you there?" Still nothing. "Come on. Are you gonna answer me?" Jim asked.

After a pause, he heard, "You told me to shut up. So which is it? Do you want me to shut up, or do you want me to give you advice?" Ethan replied.

Jim laughed. "I never thought I'd have to ask you twice for your opinion."

"Okay. Here it is. Stop talking and start doing."

"What the hell does that mean?"

"It means that you have enough information to start doing something," Ethan explained. "Start building your Customer Experience. As you build it, you'll figure out what to do next. Most of my clients spend too much time talking about what they could do and not enough time actually doing anything. You can build your full marketing experience in a few months if you get to it. Or, you can spend the next few months talking about what you should do. Your choice."

"Oh, great sage," Jim responded. "Thank you for your wisdom. Now, can you help me build it?"

"I wish I could," Ethan responded. "Our agency is swamped. We can barely handle the clients we have now, so we can't possibly take on any new work."

"So, let me get this straight. You've been giving me crap about not paying you. Now that I'm willing to pay you, you won't take my business."

"You got me. I can still bill you for these phone calls if you want. Just don't have the resources to take you on as a client."

"Okay. Just tell me how to find a good agency then."

"That's easy. Invite a few agencies to pitch for the job. Just let them know what you want from them. Then, see who has the best ideas."

Jim thanked Ethan and hung up. He started thinking about agencies that he'd invite to work on Premier's new marketing approach.

Step 5: Build a Minimally Viable Product

1. We Need to Hire an Agency

Jim met with his team the next morning. "We need to hire an agency to help us build our marketing campaign. They have to have digital experience, and they must be good at e-commerce." He explained that he wanted several agencies to pitch for the job. "I'll invite the agency I worked with at Smitty's Auto Parts, and I want each of you to think of others to invite."

"My friend from college works at a great agency," Mike said. "They've done some amazing videos for sports cars. Blow your mind kinda stuff."

"One of my podcasts featured a digital agency last week." Jenny added. "They were in a story about advanced analytics."

"Yawn." Mike opened his mouth and tapped his hand on it. "Maybe we could use their advanced analytics to help martial arts instructors go to sleep after a long day at the gym."

Lisa looked up from her notebook. "Actually, it's quite interesting. Companies are using advanced analytics to find new ways to get people to their online stores."

Mike made an exaggerated snoring sound.

Jenny ignored Mike. "I can look for agencies online. I'm sure we can find sites with some agency ratings and reviews."

The team agreed to spend the next few days looking for potential agencies. They read online articles, asked colleagues in other companies, and called agencies that were listed in marketing directories.

After a few days, they identified four agencies to include in their process. They wrote the following brief and sent it to each of the agencies:

Request-for-Proposal Brief

Thank you for agreeing to meet with us as we look for a new digital agency. We'd like you to give us an overview of your capabilities, examples of your work, and a description of how you'd approach the following project:

Business Challenges:
- *Many shoppers are purchasing sporting goods online, but Premier Sporting Goods doesn't have an online presence.*
- *We'd like to develop a campaign to drive awareness for a new brand of sports equipment that we're launching.*
- *We'd also like to develop an e-commerce strategy for selling our new products online.*

Timing:
- *July 20: present agency capabilities*
- *August 1: finalize agency selection; begin designing campaign*
- *October 1: finalize campaign elements*
- *November 1: launch campaign; start selling products online*

Presentation Format:
- *30 minutes: present capabilities and examples of your work*
- *15 minutes: show us your approach to our business challenges*
- *15 minutes: answer questions from our team*

To schedule your presentation, please contact Barbara Gaines at bgains@premiersportinggoodscorp.com.

Within a few days, all four agencies accepted the invitation and scheduled their presentations.

2. All in Favor, Say Aye

On the day of the presentations, agencies were scheduled every two hours, which allowed one hour for each presentation and one hour for Jim's team to evaluate each agency. The first presentation began at 9 a.m.

When Jim entered the conference room that morning, he saw his team and about a dozen agency people. "Hey, Jim!" he heard as he walked into the room. "It's great to see you again." It was Don Marshall, Senior VP of Client Services at Sizzle Media.

Jim greeted Don, and after a round of introductions, Don started the presentation. "With Sizzle Media, you'll get the power of over two thousand team members with extensive expertise in insights, strategy, planning, and media. We have offices worldwide, and we're known for our high-quality campaigns that win the most prestigious advertising awards."

Don's team rushed through forty-five minutes of content, including their company history, a list of awards they'd won, and examples of their television ads. They then spent fifteen minutes showing their ideas for Premier's new product launch, which included a series of extravagant ads with well-known celebrities.

Don concluded with, "I think you'll agree that we have the expansive resources needed to create a campaign that you'll be proud of."

Jim concluded by saying, "Since we're out of time, we'll just call you if we have any questions."

Jim thanked the Sizzle Media team and ushered them to the door. After they left, he turned to his team and asked, "What do you think?"

Jenny started. "Honestly, I'm exhausted. I feel like I've been presented at for the last hour. They didn't even pause to ask our opinion on anything. I mean, their resources are impressive, but I feel like they'd just give us what they give every other client, and we wouldn't get anything unique."

"I have to admit," Jim said, "they pitched the exact same idea to me when I was at Smitty's. At least they didn't tell you guys what the budget would be."

Jenny asked, "Since you brought it up, what would the budget be?"

Jim responded, "$1 million for production costs, 2 million for the celebrities, and 10 million for the media spend."

The group agreed that Sizzle was not a good fit.

***

The next agency was Q Designs. They were represented by four thin, impeccably dressed men in designer suits and stylish glasses. Their presentation focused on their cutting-edge approach, which they illustrated using ads they created for perfume brands, jewelry companies, and luxury automobiles. They bragged about being on the forefront of fashion trends with their team of world-class designers.

After the presentation ended and the Q Design team left the room, Mike led with his feedback. "My college friend said they were big time, but that's not what I expected. They might be okay for luxury brands, but not for us. Their ads didn't even explain the products. They just showed fashion models with pouty faces and skimpy clothes." He paused, then added, "While I like skimpy clothes, I don't see how it'll help us sell our gear."

The group agreed that Q Designs was also not a fit.

***

Next, four representatives from Mystic Creative Cooperative entered the room. They were dressed in t-shirts, jeans, and flip-flops. After brief introductions, they started taping pieces of paper all over the conference room walls. Each piece of paper included an idea for a marketing campaign. They presented over one hundred ideas in rapid-fire succession. As they presented, they occasionally stopped and wrote something on a new piece of paper, which they added to the collection on the walls.

After they left the room, Lisa weighed in. "No! They are the opposite of *focus*. We'd never get anything done with them constantly adding new ideas and re-thinking their approach." The team agreed. Mystic was out.

***

Jim turned to Barbara and asked, "Who's next?"

"Agile Solutions," she responded. "They've been the most inquisitive of the agencies. After we sent them the brief, they followed up with about a dozen emails and phone calls. They asked all kinds of questions about our target audience and our new brand's positioning."

"Well," Jim said with a sigh, "bring 'em in. I hope they're better than the others we've seen today."

Barbara went to the lobby and came back with a woman and a man who looked like young college professors. "Hi, I'm Amy Brown from Agile Solutions," said the woman who entered the room first.

"And I'm Ben Mathis," said the man who walked in behind her. "Before we get started, can each of you introduce yourselves and tell us what you do here at Premier?" Ben asked.

As the Premier people introduced themselves, Amy asked each of them a follow-up question about their role. Ben and Amy then summarized the information that Barbara had sent them about the project.

"We understand you're launching a new line of sparring gear," Ben said.

Amy continued with, "and you'd like to market it to martial arts instructors."

"We really like your brand positioning around focus," Ben added.

"And we can do some cool things with that positioning using digital media," Amy said.

Jenny asked, "Do you always do that?"

Ben and Amy replied in unison, "Do what?"

"Finish each other's sentences," Jenny said.

"Sorry," Amy responded. "We've been working together for years."

"And we tend to finish each other's thoughts," Ben added.

They looked at each other and chuckled. Then, they engaged Jim's team in a discussion about the research that Amy and Ben did online. That research included assessments of online stores that sold sporting goods, as well as interviews with a few martial arts instructors.

About thirty minutes into the discussion, Amy and Ben described the approach they would take for the project. They explained that Agile Solutions would assign a team of four or five people to build a prototype campaign and e-commerce experience. That team would test a series of ad messages in a variety of media environments to see which ads would be most effective.

They explained that their internal graphic designer and videographer could quickly generate banner ads, social media posts, and short videos. They would then buy small media placements to find out which ads would drive the most traffic to e-commerce sites where products would be sold. They could also build variations of e-commerce content to see which content led to the highest purchase rates.

"Here's how it works." Ben opened his laptop and showed the team a digital dashboard that looked like two high-tech maps of bustling cities. "Each of these lines represents a user navigating through these two versions of an online store."

"Each gray line represents a user who hasn't left the site yet," Amy said. "If that user buys something, the line will turn green. If they leave without buying anything, the line will turn red. As you can see, the map on the right has more green lines." Amy pointed at the screen. "This means more people are making purchases on that site design. We use this information to constantly update the store designs, keeping elements that lead to more purchases, and dropping elements that lead to users leaving without buying anything."

At the end of the hour, Jim said, "Do you mind staying a little longer? I'd like to hear more about your approach."

Amy and Ben spent another two hours showing examples of their capabilities that included continuously testing and improving the creative elements of digital campaigns. They also showed a variety of websites they created for clients. For each site, they explained how their team refined the pages based on their analysis of traffic patterns.

Finally, around 6 p.m., Ben said, "One more thing."

"We like to work on-site," Amy said.

Ben added, "We'd like to bring four or five of our people to your office so we have easy access to your team."

Jim said, "That's not a problem. We've been down-sizing, so we have plenty of space." Jim looked around the room at his team members, then back at Amy. "We'll talk it over and give you an answer quickly." With that, Jim got up, walked Amy and Ben to the front lobby, and said goodbye.

Jim walked back into the conference room and said, "All in favor, say aye."

In unison, his team members said, "Aye!"

3. When Can You Start?

Jim called Amy and Ben the next morning. "When can you start?" he asked.

"You're in luck," Amy responded.

Ben continued, "We finished a project earlier than expected, so we're available on Monday."

The Agile Solutions team that arrived at Premier's office on Monday morning included Amy, Ben, a graphic designer, and a coding expert. They requested that someone from Premier's creative agency join their team. Jim agreed, and Cindy began working with them the next day.

Jim also assigned Mike Reed, his marketing manager, to the team. Jim instructed Mike to work full-time on the project for the next few months. Lisa and Jenny would also work with the team as insights and analytics consultants.

Mike promptly asked Jim if he could get uniforms for the team members. Jim denied that request, explaining that uniforms would not be good for the team's morale. Jim did agree to let Mike name the team. After conferring with the other members, Mike announced that the team would be called the Amazing Fokasu Team.

The team spent their first day setting up a war room in one of Premier's small conference rooms. On their second day, Lisa spent the morning showing them the insights she had gathered about the sporting goods industry. She also showed them the customer journey for martial arts gear and gave them her assessment of existing products that would be in their competitive set. Next, she reviewed the results from the surveys she gathered from martial arts instructors.

Jenny showed them how the company's supply chain would work for the martial arts gear. Team members asked questions, made comments, and took notes throughout their meetings with Lisa and Jenny.

Three days into the project, Amy and Ben scheduled a meeting with Jim and the rest of their Fokasu Team. Amy started the meeting by saying, "We have our first big decision to make. We need to decide if we start selling our gear in someone else's online store, or if we build our own site."

Jim explained that they had already made that decision. They had chosen to sell the gear on someone else's site.

"Okay." Ben nodded. "Let's reevaluate that choice."

Mike asked, "Is that a polite way of saying that you don't agree with our decision?"

Amy responded, "Not exactly. We may have capabilities that could change the decision. Before we lock in on our approach, we just want to review our options and course-correct if needed."

Ben grabbed a marker and walked over to a flip chart. "Let's go over the pros and cons of each option. Then, as a team, we'll make the decision together."

They spent over an hour weighing both options. At one point, they were in favor of using someone else's e-commerce site since it would be quicker to implement and it would already have existing traffic.

Then, they switched their perspective when they realized how easy it would be to build a site using Agile's capabilities. Plus, with their own site, they would have more control over the shopping experience. They also liked having the ability to monitor site traffic patterns and make adjustments to page layouts. In the end, they decided that building their own online store would be the better choice.

Ben summarized the discussion by saying, "Okay. We're all set. The team'll start building our online store. We can always start selling our products on existing sites later, but for now, let's focus on our own site."

***

The next day, Amy and Ben led a work session to build the team's project plan. They defined three phases:

Phase 1 involved creating a *Minimally Viable Product*. In this phase, they'd identify the minimum content and features needed to launch an online store. They'd then build the site and *qualify* it. When Mike asked what *qualify* meant, Amy explained that it involved testing the site and removing any glitches.

Phase 2 included launching the site and building traffic. It involved developing their marketing content and advertising the site to their target users. It also included continuously refining their marketing messages and media choices.

Phase 3 involved expanding their product offerings and site features. When Cindy asked how long Phase 3 would last, Ben answered, "Forever. Companies should always be expanding and refining their sites."

Cindy smiled at this. "I like your agency model. It's brilliant to include a phase that lasts forever."

Amy laughed. Then, she wrote the following diagram on one of the conference room's whiteboards.

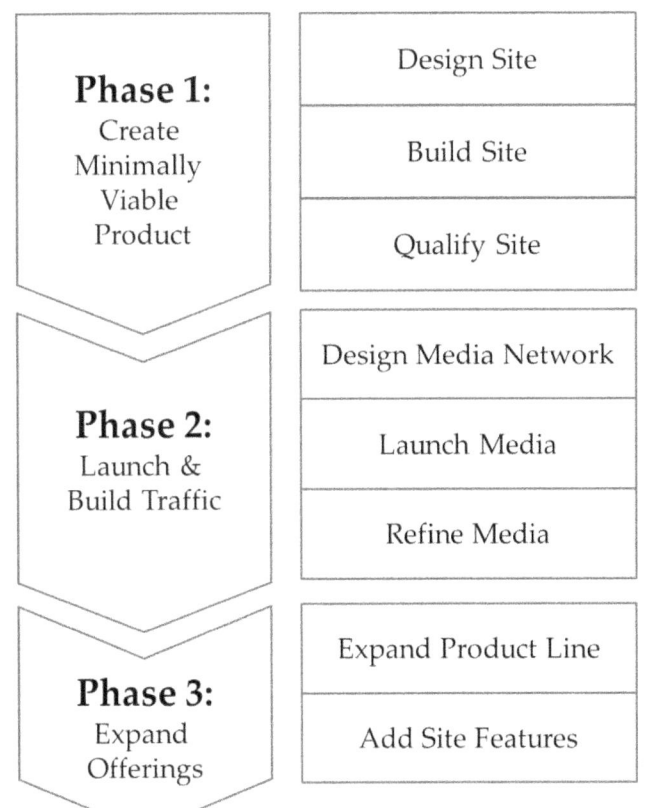

"This diagram will be here from now on so we can keep track of our progress. While Phase 3 will last forever, Phases 1 and 2 will go very quickly."

"How quickly?" Mike asked.

Jenny said, "Jim has a presentation to a group of investment bankers in less than three months. Do you think we could have a functioning site by then?"

"Absolutely," Ben answered. "We'll have a functioning site in about two months. In three months, we'll have a steady flow of orders and we'll be making some real money from the site."

Cindy's jaw dropped. "I've been working for marketing agencies for years, and I've never seen anything get designed and start deliver results that quickly."

"Welcome to the digital age," Amy responded.

4. Today, We'll Design Our Online Store

The next morning, Ben taped a giant piece of paper to a wall in their war room. Across the top of the paper, he had written ONLINE STORE.

He called the team together and announced, "Today, we'll design our online store. We'll identify all the possible sections for the site. Then, we'll group and prioritize those sections."

"Here's a stack of sticky notes for each of you," Amy said. "As you say an idea, write it on a sticky and put it on the wall. I'll start. I suggest Catalog." She wrote down *Catalog* and stuck the paper to the wall.

Mike went next. "How about Videos?" he suggested. He wrote *Videos* on a sticky and added it to the wall.

Cindy said, "Should we have a Shopping Cart section?"

"You bet," Amy answered.

The group continued generating ideas for about an hour. They spent another hour discussing, prioritizing, adding, and removing ideas. When they were finished, the following outline for a website was on the wall:

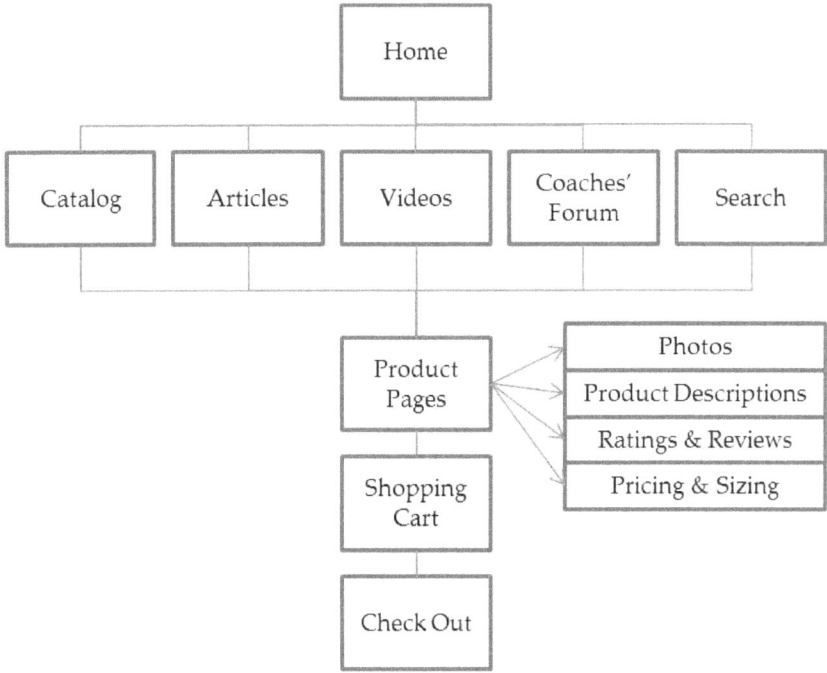

Ben said, "Great job team! Now, that's our roadmap."

Amy turned to Cindy and asked, "Can you have your creative team show us options for the site's look-and-feel?"

Cindy answered quickly, "Absolutely. I'll show you several options in a few days."

"Great," Ben responded. "Our graphic designer and coder will start building the wireframes. Then, they'll add the content as we get it ready for them."

The team spent the next week building a beta version of the online store. As a starting point, the Agile team used a turnkey e-commerce platform that they built for another client. Then, they modified it to match the Fokasu Team's design.

While they were working on the site, Olivia Whitten secured a contract with her supplier in China for the purchase of sparring gear. The supplier shipped the gear to one of Premier's warehouses in the United States so the team could start using that inventory for their initial wave of online orders.

5. Let's Do an A-B Test

A few days later, Cindy presented creative designs for the team to consider. They quickly narrowed the options to two territories. Mike and Barbara preferred a design with dark, intricate graphics. Jenny and Lisa preferred a design with lighter, simpler graphics.

With the team split between the two options, Amy broke the deadlock. "We don't have to choose. Let's mock up a few pages and have the instructors decide."

"Yep," Ben said. "Let's do an A-B test."

"What's an A-B test?" Jenny asked.

Mike responded, "It's a test that Amy and Ben invented. That's why they call it A-B. For Amy and Ben. Get it?"

"Actually . . ." Amy gave a mock-wince and shook her head. "No. We'll have one group of instructors see Option A and another group see Option B. We'll measure their behavior and see which group is more likely to make purchases."

Lisa said she could recruit martial arts instructors for online research, and within a week they could be testing the two options. Cindy worked with her agency to create graphics for both design territories while the Agile team rushed to get a draft of the site ready. A week later, they were testing the designs with instructors.

***

When the results were in, Lisa called a team meeting and invited Jim to join. "We have a winner," she announced.

"Go Team A!" blurted out Mike.

"Well . . . actually," Lisa answered softly as if proceeding with caution, "instructors preferred Option B. In our post-interviews, the people who saw Option B said the site was clear and easy to navigate. The people who saw Option A said they were distracted by the busyness of the site."

"Boo!" Mike responded. He raised his hands with both thumbs pointing down. "It looks like we'll have a boring site."

Jenny replied, "The goal of the site isn't to entertain people. It's to sell products, and Option B does a better job of that."

"That's right," Ben said. "Throughout this project, we'll use A-B testing to assess which options lead to better results. It's a lot faster and more accurate than the typical approach for evaluating options."

"What do you mean by the typical approach?" Mike asked.

Jenny responded, "Typically, the highest ranking team member decides, or we just debate indefinitely and never make a decision. As the lowest ranking team member, I really like A-B testing, especially when it says that I'm right and Mike's wrong."

***

After another week of testing and refinement, the team had a site that they were ready to show Jim.

Amy, Ben, and Mike walked into Jim's office, and Mike announced, "Our online store is ready for you to see."

"Great!" Jim said. "Show me."

Mike handed Jim an iPad. "Here you go."

Jim looked at the site, and he was amazed at how professional it was. "Wow! This is great! When can people start shopping on it?"

"Right now," Ben replied. "We thought you should have the honor of being our first customer. Just go through the site and make a purchase."

"We'll be watching you," Mike said, "so hopefully you'll get it right."

Jim grinned and started tapping on the screen. "I like the navigation. It's easy to find what I'm looking for." After a short pause, he continued. "I'm ordering my gear now, and I'm not sure what size to get. How do I know whether I'm a Medium, a Large, or an Extra Large?"

"Good point," Amy replied. "We'll have our designer create a chart so people can match their measurements to the proper size descriptions."

"For this shopping trip," Mike added, "just pick Extra Large."

"I'm offended by that comment." Jim glared at Mike with an exaggerated frown.

Amy added, "Mike, it's not good to tell your boss's boss that he's extra large."

"Well, uh, maybe I meant he's big . . . like, body-builder big," Mike replied.

"Too late," Jim said with a smile. "Damage is done. You're on coffee duty for a week."

Jim looked back at the iPad and began tapping on the screen again. He pulled out his credit card and started entering information into the site. When he finished his purchase, he said, "Very nice first draft. Here are a couple of things I noticed. There were too many clicks needed to get to the ordering screen, and the site didn't tell me when my gear would arrive."

"Other than that, Mrs. Lincoln, how was the play?" Mike asked.

"Sorry," Jim said. "I didn't mean to imply that the site came to a tragic end. I really like it. As a first draft, I'm extremely impressed."

"This is exactly the kind of feedback we want," Amy said. We all need to scour the site and find ways to improve it. We'll get started on the measurement chart; we'll add the delivery info; and we'll reduce the number of clicks needed to place an order."

Ben added, "I'll send everyone a link to an online chat room and tell them to post suggestions there. Our team'll go through those posts and make adjustments to the site."

After Amy, Ben, and Mike left Jim's office, Jim sat in his chair and smiled. He was astounded by the progress his team had made, and he was looking forward to updating Premier's executive team. Fortunately, there was an executive staff meeting the next day, so he could share the good news then. He didn't realize that he was about to get a very unexpected reaction from his counterparts.

6. Just Stay out of Our Way

As Jim was about to go into the executive staff meeting, he thought about his first few months at Premier. He spent the first month settling into his new job. Then, there was that chaotic day when everything changed; the day when he learned Walt Bigman signed a deal with another company; the day when Titan Supercenters declared bankruptcy; the day when Patrick Feldman resigned.

Now, he had completed three months on the job. It had been the most challenging, most invigorating months of his career. He couldn't wait to tell his counterparts about the progress his team had made over the past few weeks.

When he walked into the room, Francis and Sam glared at him. Olivia smiled and said, "Good morning, Jim. Come sit next to me."

As Jim sat down, Ed Baxter entered the room and said, "Let's get started. The meeting with our investment bankers is less than two months away, so I want to hear what each of you has been doing to prepare for it. Sam, you first."

Sam cleared his throat. "I've got a great plan. Since Jim blew the deal with Bigman, we'll need something huge to make a splash. I can get Bernie Landau for a week of golf with the top executives of our best retail partners. Get this. We can spend the entire week with them in Hawaii. They'll love it! Just think how much they'll give us in exchange for spending time with a golf legend like Bernie."

"Interesting," Ed said. "How much will it cost?"

"Less than you might think. We can book the most exclusive golf resort for under a million dollars. Travel expenses for everyone will be about half a million. And Bernie's agent said we can get him for a million, which would cover the entire week. If we put another half-million into gifts, catering, and guest speakers, we can do the entire event for around three million bucks."

Ed asked, "Do you think the executives will take a week out of their schedules for this?"

"You bet," Sam said with a wave of his hand. "We'll call it an industry conference and get a few fancy guest speakers so it'll seem like something their boards of directors would support. Hell, we might even get a few board members to come."

"You've got seven weeks to put the proposal together," Ed said. "Then, I want you to share it with our investment bankers. If they like the idea, I'm okay with it."

He turned to Olivia. "What about you?"

"Jim and I are working on something together," she said.

Francis rolled his eyes. "Why does that worry me?"

Ignoring him, Olivia continued. "We're testing a new line of martial arts equipment that we can sell online. Jim can have our e-commerce site up and running in a few weeks."

"Oh no!" Sam said. "No. Absolutely not. You're not selling anything directly to consumers. Competing with our retail partners would jeopardize everything."

"Do we have any contracts with them that prohibit us from selling directly to consumers?" Jim asked.

"That's not the point." Sam shook his head dismissively. "It's not about contracts. It's about relationships."

"Don't most of our retailers sell their own brands of sporting goods?" Olivia asked.

Francis asked, "What's your point?"

"We're already in competition with them," Olivia answered. "When they started selling their own brands of equipment, they started competing with us."

"That's irrelevant," Sam said.

"Actually, it's a good point," Ed said. "We're in competition with them whether we like it or not."

Olivia and Jim explained their plan to launch a new line of sparring gear and market it online. They explained their research with martial arts instructors and their work with Agile Solutions.

"I didn't authorize any of this!" Francis shouted. "Big projects like this require my approval, and I didn't approve any of it." He pointed a finger at his sister. "Shut it down now."

"Actually," Olivia replied calmly, "total project costs have been under $500,000, so I'm authorized to pay for that amount out of my budget . . . without your approval."

"Well, you still need to shut it down," Sam said. "If our customers hear about this, they'll never give us another display in their stores again. Plus, who knows how many of our secrets those agency people are stealing. How could you let them into our office?"

Jim explained that every Agile team member signed a nondisclosure agreement. Plus, they were only seeing information about the martial arts gear, so they wouldn't have access to any proprietary information.

Finally, Ed ended the debate by saying, "I don't see anything wrong with what Olivia and Jim are doing." He turned to them and said, "Keep going. I want to see an update in six weeks, so I can decide if we share your ideas with the investment bankers."

"This is stupid!" Sam said. "You're wasting your time, and you're gonna regret it." He stood up, stormed out of the room, and slammed the door on his way out.

"I agree." Francis scoffed. "There's no way a project like this will pay out. You'll sink a fortune into it with nothing to show in the end. I'll have nothing to do with this."

"Good!" Olivia said. "Just stay out of our way, and we'll be fine."

Ed looked at Olivia and wondered if his little sister could pull this off. He secretly hoped she would prove Sam and Francis wrong.

7. We Have a Revolution on Our Hands

Jim and Olivia debated whether to tell the Fokasu Team about the argument with Sam and Francis. In the end, they decided to tell them everything. They thought it would motivate the team to know that Sam and Francis were trying to stop them.

At Jim's staff meeting the next day, he told the team about Sam's and Francis's reactions. When they heard the news, the team members were energized. "Let's prove 'em wrong!" Mike shouted.

"For once, I agree with Mike," Jenny said. We've been playing by their rules too long. How dare they try to shut us down?"

"I think we've got a revolution on our hands," Jim said. "Now, let's focus this energy in a constructive way. I don't want anyone causing any trouble with Sales or Finance. They're still our partners, and we don't want to fight with them."

The team agreed. They would work harder than ever on their online store, but they would still be respectful to everyone else in the company.

Amy and Ben just looked at each other and smiled. They loved working with a motivated team, and they just got a giant burst of motivation thanks to Sam and Francis.

As the meeting ended, Jim asked Lisa to stay behind. "Lisa, you've been so quiet," he said. "What's on your mind?"

"Honestly, I'm a bit hurt," she answered. "It bothers me when people don't believe in what I'm doing. I've been dealing with that my whole career. Everyone thinks insights people don't provide any value, but I think we do."

"You absolutely do," Jim said. "Think about what we're doing here. This all started when you convinced us to ask some tough questions. You've been leading us to a completely new business model, and you've gotten this entire team to believe in what we're doing. You've done it in your own quiet way, but you've done it!"

"Huh. I never thought of it that way," Lisa said pursing her lips as if to stop herself from smiling. "Do you really think I've made a difference?"

Jim answered with a question of his own. "Do you remember that meeting when you suggested that we ask some questions before we decided what to do? Do you remember what we were talking about before you made that suggestion?"

Lisa didn't say anything.

Jim continued. "We were dangerously close to letting Mike start a radio station sponsored by Premier Sports. What was it? The WWMD Show, the voice of sports fans everywhere."

Lisa smiled.

"What did WWMD stand for anyway?" Jim asked.

Lisa responded, "What Would Mike Do."

"Oh yeah," Jim said. He paused. "Lisa, we'd be lost without you. Every step of the way, you've nudged us in a better directly. You should never feel like you're not making a difference."

In a soft voice, Lisa said, "That's a double negative."

"Ugh. Okay. Let me say it this way. As long as you speak out, you'll always make a difference, especially on this team. When we're stuck, everyone looks to you. They know that you're the smartest person in the room . . . and they really value that. Keep pushing us, and keep challenging us if you feel like we're moving in the wrong direction. You hear me?"

"Okay," she said. "Thanks."

8. We Need Real Users to Test the Site

Ben, Amy, and Mike met with Jim to discuss next steps. "We're ready to qualify the site," Amy said.

"What does that mean?" Jim asked.

"It means we'll test the site with actual users to see what doesn't work," Ben said. "It also means that we'll see if the site leads our shoppers to make purchases."

"Yeah, but what do you mean, *see what doesn't work*?" Jim asked. "I tested the site, and everything worked fine."

"We can't test everything ourselves," Amy replied. "We can't possibly think of every action that users will take when they're on the site. We need real users to test the site. They'll try things that we'd never think of, and that's where we'll find the glitches. We just need a big group of martial arts instructors to test with."

"I have an idea," Jim said. "There's a taekwondo tournament this weekend, and we might be able to get a booth there. We could get instructors to try the site at the tournament."

Jim called the tournament organizers and confirmed that they still had available booths. He reserved one, and he invited the full Fokasu Team to see the testing process in person.

At the tournament, the team offered free cups of coffee and free sparring gear to any instructor willing to test the site. They had over thirty people spend an average of ten minutes on the site. While most features worked as planned, the instructors found two major issues.

With one instructor, his shopping cart emptied every time he hit the Back button. Amy took a few notes, which she sent to her coding expert.

Several instructors discovered that they couldn't find the menu bar when they accessed the site from their phones. Ben noticed that those instructors all had a type of phone that was different from the phones the Fokasu team members had used to test the site. He captured that issue, and he sent a note to the team's graphic designer.

After they packed up the booth, the team members compared notes. They noticed that instructors seemed very pleased with the site. Other than the two technical issues, instructors gave them very positive feedback. Most of the instructors even agreed to participate in follow-up interviews once they received the gear that they had ordered.

"We'll have the technical issues resolved by Tuesday, and we'll be ready to move into Phase 2," Amy announced.

Step 6: Launch the Online Store and Campaign

1. We'll Design Our Media Network

The next day, Ben taped another giant piece of paper to a wall near the paper labeled ONLINE STORE. Across the top of the new paper, he had written MEDIA NETWORK and just below that, he had written AUDIENCE, MEDIA, and CONTENT.

He called the team together and announced, "Today, we'll design our Media Network. We'll start with this shopping process that your team created before hiring us." He taped the following diagram next to the MEDIA NETWORK paper.

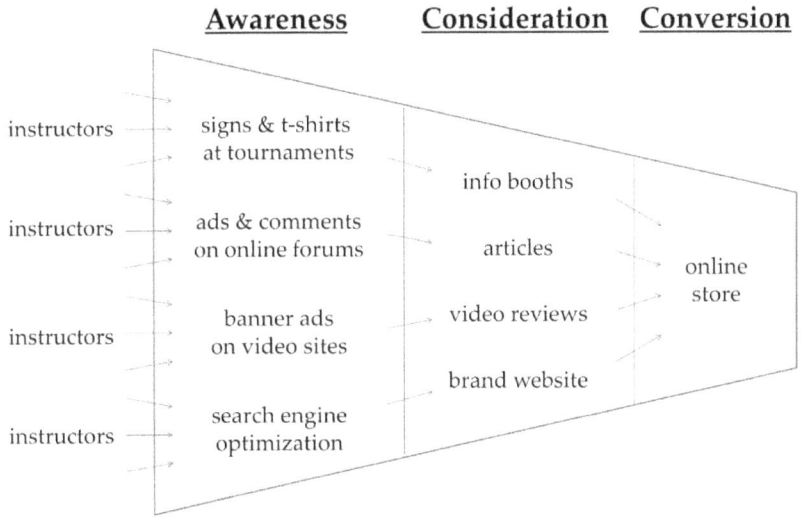

Amy continued, "We'll identify every possible way to communicate to our target audiences. Then, we'll prioritize those ideas."

Ben pointed to each column on the chart. "AUDIENCE means who should see your message? MEDIA means where will they see it. And CONTENT means what will they see. When we're done generating ideas, we'll prioritize the audience groups, the media, and the content that will be most effective."

"Here's your sticky notes," Amy said, handing out several note pads. "I'll go first. For the AUDIENCE column, *Sports Bloggers*." She wrote *Sports Bloggers* on a note and stuck it to the wall.

Ben went next. "For the CONTENT column, *Banner Ads*." He added his note.

"In the MEDIA column, I recommend we advertise on sports radio shows." Mike said.

The team continued to generate ideas for over an hour. They spent another hour discussing and prioritizing the ideas. When they finished, the wall looked like the following diagram.

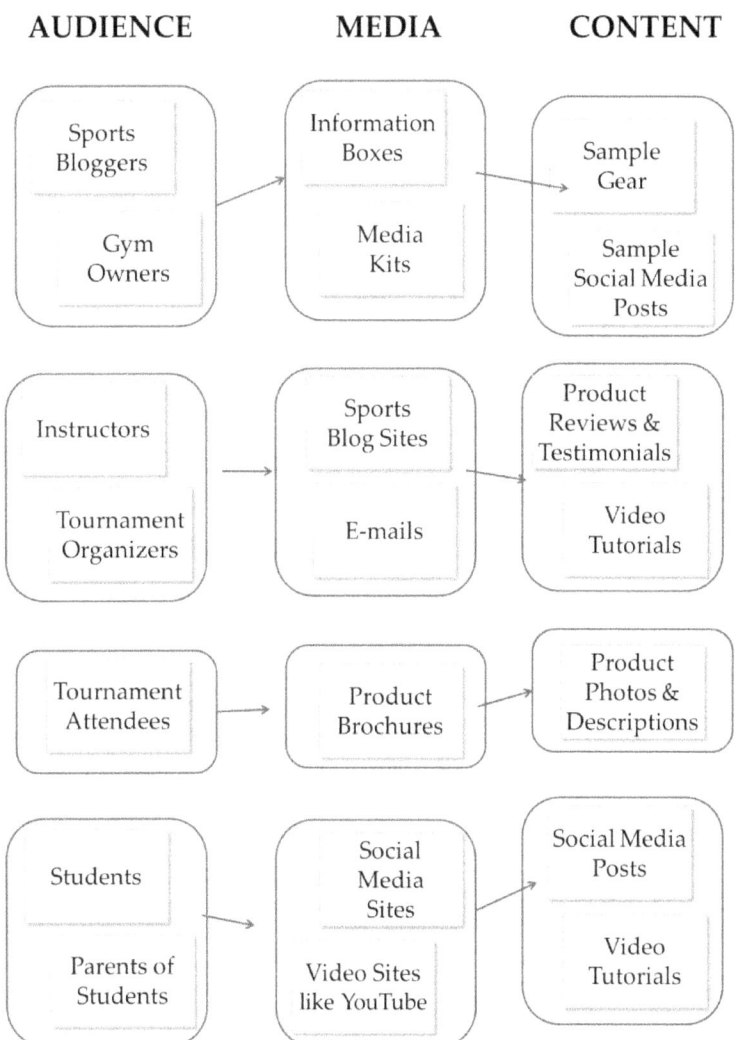

"Okay," Amy said. "That's our project list. Now, let's choose our top one or two priorities."

After another discussion, the team decided to start with sports bloggers and gym owners who had martial arts sites. They agreed that focusing on these people would give them the best ability to reach a broad audience of instructors who made the actual purchase decisions.

Next, they agreed to communicate directly with instructors. They decided to delay communicating with tournament attendees, students, and parents since they weren't as involved in the brand selection decisions.

"Great," Ben said. "Now, about the content for bloggers and gym owners, we need to research their sites."

"Let's figure out what kind of content they include," Amy said. "Where do they get their content? How might we persuade them to post content about our brand? Stuff like that."

"Let's talk with our panel of instructors to see which blogs they look at," Lisa said. "We can also ask them who selects the content for their gyms' websites."

2. Every Star Has to Start Somewhere

Over the next few days, the team gathered insights about bloggers and gym websites. They found forty site hosts who might be interested in content about the Fokasu gear.

In their research, they learned that most of those sites were hosted by people who enjoyed trying out martial arts gear. The site hosts also liked to get digital content to post on their sites.

Ben said, "We can send them media kits with information about our gear."

"Should we A-B test the content in our media kits to see what's most effective?" Mike asked.

"Good idea. You learn quickly." Amy said.

The team put together media kits that included a memory stick with sample articles for the bloggers. It also included product demo videos that the team had gotten from their equipment supplier in China.

Mike recorded separate voice-overs for the videos since the original voice-overs were in Chinese.

All twenty of the A kits included a set of medium-sized sparring gear. That was the most popular size, so the team hoped it would fit many of the site hosts. All twenty of the B kits included a gift card with a code to order gear from the Fokasu online store free of charge. That way, the site hosts could select the size that would fit them.

As the team shipped the media kits, Amy said, "Now we'll monitor the sites to see if any of them post articles about our gear."

While they waited, the team generated social media posts and emails. They tested each message with their panel of instructors to determine the most compelling wording, graphics, and video content. They opened Fokasu accounts on Facebook, Twitter, Instagram, and other social media sites that instructors mentioned during their interviews.

Within a week, they started seeing activity. Six of the bloggers posted articles about their gear: four from the A group and two from the B group. "Okay," Mike said. "Let's send out more of the A kits."

"Not so fast," Ben said. "We should wait a little longer before we make that call. Since the B group had to order the gear separately, it might take them longer to post anything."

"That's right," Amy said. "Let's look to see if any of the B group ordered gear." She opened their software program that tracked online orders. It indicated that forty-six orders had been placed.

"Five of those orders were placed when we were testing the site, and thirty-one were from the instructors who ordered gear at the tournament," Ben said. "That might mean that ten orders came from our B group." He pulled up the order details and cross-referenced them with the blogger list. They all matched.

"That's great news," Amy said. "It means that half of the kits led to people ordering their free gear. It looks like all of them should receive their gear in a few days, so we just have to watch and see if they post anything."

In the meantime, the team read the six posted articles. All six were positive, and all of them included either a photo or a video from the media kit. Mike was thrilled to see that three of the sites included the videos with his voiceovers.

"I'm famous!" he shouted.

"Calm down, Mike," Jenny said. "These blogger sites aren't exactly mainstream media."

"Well, every star has to start somewhere," Mike responded. "Hey, can we post my videos to YouTube?" he asked Amy.

"Sure," she answered. "Let's create a YouTube channel and upload the videos now."

"While we're at it," Ben added, "let's upload them to Vimeo, DailyMotion, and other sites. We'll do it on one condition."

"What's that?" Mike asked.

Amy replied, "You don't call them *your* videos. You may be the voice talent, but we'd like to think of them as *our* videos."

"Aw, come on," Mike responded. "Let me enjoy my 15 minutes."

Over the next few weeks, the team continued to monitor the blogs, send out more media kits, and make adjustments based on their observations. Within a month of the time they shipped their first kits, they had over five hundred orders for their gear.

Their biggest break came when Ninja World Gyms posted a review of Fokasu gear on their company's website. With over a thousand instructors in the Ninja World network, the review gave Fokasu exposure to people who made purchasing decisions for over a hundred thousand students. Within days of the post, over three hundred orders were placed. The team sent another wave of media kits with gift cards to hundreds of gyms, and the orders continued to come in.

3. That's a Bullseye

Amy and Ben met with Jim to give him a project update, and they told him about the progress they had made. They also explained their plans to test a wide variety of ad messages for their upcoming digital marketing campaign.

"I appreciate all the work you're doing," Jim said, "but it seems like we'll be testing too many things. Wouldn't it be better to pick one message and stick with it?"

"Not really," Amy answered. "Can we move this meeting to a different location? I'd like to show you something."

Jim looked at Amy with a puzzled expression. "Okay. Where do you want to go?"

She responded, "There's a bar down the street from here. Do you know Danny's Pub?"

"Yeah," Jim said. "But what does a pub have to do with our advertising message?"

Amy gave Ben a sly grin. "Trust us. Meet us there in ten minutes."

***

When Jim arrived, he saw Amy and Ben near the back of the bar. Amy waved him over and handed him a few darts.

As Jim took the darts, he asked, "What are these for?"

Ben motioned to a nearby dartboard. "Try to hit a bullseye."

Jim frowned. He turned to the dartboard and threw one of the darts. It hit the wall next to the dartboard and fell to the floor.

Ben picked up the dart. "Now, put your right foot in front of your left foot, and put your weight on your right foot. Try to hit the bullseye again."

Jim did as Ben instructed and threw the next dart. It hit the outer edge of the dartboard and stuck there.

"Good," Amy said. "Now, hold the dart out in front of you, and point it directly at the center of the target before you throw it."

Jim did as she said and threw the next dart. It hit a little closer to the center.

Ben smiled at Amy. "Now, hold your left hand on top of your head as you throw the next dart."

Jim did that, and his next dart hit the wall.

"Okay," Amy said. "Put your left hand at your side when you throw the next dart." Amy and Ben kept giving Jim instructions, and Jim played along. After about a dozen variations, Jim was getting closer to the bullseye.

Jim turned to Amy. "I still don't get what this has to do with our ad campaign."

Amy handed a dart to Ben. "Watch this."

Ben walked next to Jim, turned toward the dartboard, and took a deep breath. He held the dart at eye level in front of him, pointing it directly toward the dartboard. He moved his hand forward in a smooth motion, and the dart flew to the target. It stuck in the dartboard . . . in the exact center.

Amy turned to Jim and smiled. "That's a bullseye."

"Beginner's luck," Jim said.

Amy handed another dart to Ben.

Ben went through the same ritual and let the next dart fly.

Amy didn't even look at the target. Her eyes stayed locked on Jim. "Bullseye," she said. She was right. The dart was stuck to the center of the target, right next to Ben's first dart.

Jim turned to Amy. "How does he do that?"

Amy answered with a question. "Jim, how many different variations did you try when you were throwing your darts?"

"Maybe a dozen," Jim answered.

"Well, Ben has tried hundreds of variations to his technique. When he tries something that gets him closer to the bullseye, he knows he's on the right track. When he tries something that doesn't work, he immediately sees the result on the dartboard."

Ben turned to Jim. "That's what we'll be doing with our ad testing. We'll be trying different messages to figure out what works."

Jim smiled. "I see. Just like you've perfected your dart-throwing technique through trial and error, we're perfecting our ads. But do we really need to try so many variations?"

"The more options we try," Amy said, "the more we can refine our approach. Each variation tells us if we're getting closer to meeting our goals."

Ben added, "We just need to measure each thing we try to see if it works."

"I get it," Jim said. "Just like every change I made when I was throwing darts either got me closer to the bullseye or further from it, every change to our ads will do the same."

"That's right," Amy said. "Now, let's get some beers and get back to improving your dart skills."

4. Even a Blind Squirrel Finds a Nut

In the next Fokasu team meeting, Ben showed the team a tracking spreadsheet with data for every element of their marketing campaign. With that spreadsheet, they could see which tactics were generating the most traffic to their online store.

Over the next few weeks, the team conducted A-B tests on a wide variety of marketing messages to determine which content generated the highest click-through rates. They learned that messages emphasizing benefits to students were most effective, so they shifted their campaign to those messages.

The team modified their online store frequently to see which designs resulted in the highest purchase rates. They found that the simplest site designs usually led to the highest likelihood of purchases. When the site was too complex, users seemed to lose interest before they bought anything.

"I don't understand," Cindy said. "I've always been told that we want to maximize the time people spend on sites. Wouldn't that suggest our site should be more complex so it will hold people's attention longer?"

"It's actually the opposite," Ben replied. "The longer people spend on a site, the less likely they are to make purchases."

"You want them to complete their purchase transactions as quickly as possible. That's why the best online stores now include a one-click purchase option. It shortens the number of steps in the purchase process," Amy said.

"So, maybe we should test a one-click purchase feature," Mike said.

"Yeah, why not?" Ben responded. "For things that don't require specific sizing, we can do that. Let's add it to the gear bags screen and see what happens."

Mike straightened his shoulders. "You're welcome."

"Even a blind squirrel finds a nut once in a while." Jenny said, making everyone laugh.

Jim asked the team to summarize the campaign results for him. "Ed's given me the go ahead to show our plan to the investment bankers. The meeting's in a few days, and I'll be pitching for that $5 million prize. I need every bit of information we have to show that our online store is working."

Jenny led the analytical project with Lisa contributing the shopper insights. Cindy, Amy, and Ben worked on summarizing the campaign elements. Mike found a way to stream the presentation from Jim's phone to the TV screen in the main conference room. By the day of the investors meeting, Jim was ready.

5. We Didn't Get the $5 Million

"Welcome to our quarterly investors meeting," Ed Baxter said to the room full of investment bankers. "As many of you know, our plans for an initial public offering hit a speed bump a few months ago when our biggest retail customer went out of business. Today, we'll show you two plans to regain our momentum and get us back on track for the IPO. First, I'll turn it over to Sam Baxter, our chief sales officer, and Francis Baxter, our chief financial officer."

Sam stood up and told the audience that they were in for a treat. He clicked through a PowerPoint presentation filled with beautiful photos of a golf resort in Hawaii. He told the investment bankers about his plan to host a prestigious golf tournament for their top retail customers and investors.

"I've hosted tournaments like this in the past, and our customers always line up to attend. When we implement this plan," he said, "I'll make sure each of you gets an invitation. I can even give you an opportunity to meet Bernie Landau. He's my favorite golf legend, and I'm sure he's yours too."

Francis presented several charts showing how the tournament would lead to bigger displays in stores and higher sales for the company.

When the presentation was over, the investment bankers were silent. "That must be a good sign," Sam said. "Francis and I must have answered all your questions."

Ed stood up and said, "Next, Jim Harrison, our chief marketing officer, will show you our second plan."

Jim thanked the investment bankers for their time and support. "Over the past few months, we've embarked on a new chapter for our company," he said confidently. "Through extensive market research, we've identified martial arts equipment as our next big growth opportunity. Olivia Whitten, our chief operations officer, has done a wonderful job securing a supply of the most innovative martial arts sparring gear in the world. She negotiated an exclusive contract for this gear in the United States, so we'll have better products than any of our competitors."

He continued by telling the bankers about the size of the market opportunity. He then demonstrated the gear for the audience and showed how it was superior to the leading competitors.

"Now, if you'll turn your attention to the screen, let me show you our marketing plan." He touched his phone, and the screen lit up with a series of videos, social media posts, and blogger articles. "As you can see, we've created a high-impact campaign based on input we received from the people who make the purchase decisions. All this media directs the shoppers to our online store, where we make it simple for them to purchase our products." He tapped his phone again, and the Fokasu online store appeared on the screen. "Let me walk you through the site."

He showed the audience the online store and placed an order for sparring gear in under a minute. "As you can see, the site is intuitive and leads shoppers seamlessly through the purchase process."

One of the bankers asked, "How soon will the site go live?" Another asked, "How fast do you expect to see meaningful sales?"

Jim paused, looked around the room, and said, "The site went live last month. So far, we've had over 4,000 transactions at an average of $300 per transaction. We expect to triple that number next month. By the end of next year, our sales for martial arts gear should surpass our sales for golf equipment. By the end of the following year, we project that martial arts gear will become our top-selling product line."

"How profitable will the product line be?" one of the bankers asked.

"I'm glad you asked," Jim responded. He tapped his phone again and a page appeared showing a comparison of profit margins for their baseball, football, golf, and martial arts gear. "As you can see, the martial arts equipment has a margin that's ten points higher than our other product lines. Since we use our own online store, we've eliminated most of our selling costs."

Sam cringed, and Francis shook his head.

Jim walked around the room handing gift cards to each audience member. "Here's a gift card so you can try the shopping experience yourselves. Go to FokasuGear.com, select the gear you want, and enter the code on the card when you check out."

Jim answered a few more questions before Ed interrupted. "That's all the time we have for the presentations. I'm going to ask my leadership team to step out of the room so you can talk amongst yourselves. We'll be back in an hour to hear your reaction to our two plans."

Ed and his team walked out of the conference room and into Ed's office. Sam immediately turned to Jim and said, "Well, that was brutal. They really grilled you about all your martial arts plans. While I applaud your efforts, that wasn't even close."

Jim responded, "It will be interesting to see what they say." He gave a nearly imperceptible wink to Olivia, and she gave him a very satisfied grin. Ed also gave him a nod.

About fifteen minutes later, one of the investment bankers knocked on Ed's door. "We're ready for you," he said.

"Already?" Ed asked. He and his executive team walked back into the conference room.

One of the bankers said, "We have a few more questions for Jim."

Sam let out a smug "Hmm" sound.

The banker continued, "If we invest an extra $10 million, how fast could you expand the site?"

"Would that help you add additional product lines to the online store?" another investor asked.

"I have a client that manufactures running shoes," another said. "Would you be willing to sell their products on your site?"

The questions kept coming, and Jim answered them one at a time.

Ed asked, "Do you have any questions for Sam and Francis?"

The room went silent. After an awkward pause, one of the bankers said, "No, they can go. But first, they need to promise they won't spend another penny on golf tournaments. Otherwise, we'll drop our support for your IPO."

Ed turned to Sam and said, "You and Francis may go." Ed turned back to the bankers and asked, "Do you have any more questions for Jim?"

They did. They stayed for another two hours. Eventually, Ed closed the meeting by confirming that the IPO was back on.

Each banker confirmed their support under the condition that Jim would keep expanding the online store. Jim agreed, and the meeting ended.

Jim walked out of the conference room to the war room where the Fokasu Team was waiting. His entire staff was there, along with Amy, Ben, and Cindy.

"Well?" Jenny asked as soon as he entered.

"I've got bad news," Jim responded.

His team looked at him in shock, and Jim remained silent for a long moment.

"Come on!" Mike said. "Tell us what happened."

Jim looked down at his feet. "We didn't get the $5 million."

Everyone's faces fell. The room was silent.

After a long pause, Jim looked up. Everyone stared at him as his frown turned into a mischievous grin. "We got $15 million."

The room erupted with cheering that could be heard all the way to Sam's and Francis's offices.

"Tell us all about it," Lisa demanded.

Jim recapped the entire meeting including all the key details. The team stayed late into the evening while Jim recounted the best day of his career.

After everyone had left, Jim went back to his office and called his wife. When she answered, she said, "Well, it's about time. So, tell me. How was your big presentation?"

"It was great," he responded. "I'm heading home, so I'll tell you all about it when I get there." Jim said good-bye and hung up the phone.

As he was leaving, Jim noticed that his phone's message light was on. He quickly entered his passcode and retrieved the message. It was from one of the investment bankers. "Hey, Jim. This is Ted Huffings. We met earlier today, and I'd like to talk with you about a new job. I'm a key investor in a start-up company that's looking for a new chief executive officer, and you might be the right guy for the job. Call me."

Jim smiled, hung up the phone, and thought, "Not tonight. I'm going home to celebrate with my family. Maybe I'll call Ted back tomorrow . . . or maybe not."

Conclusion

Thank you for reading this book. We hope you've enjoyed it. Here are a few of our favorite lessons from this story:

1. Look Outside Your Comfort Zone: People in established companies often look only at the world that they know best. The leaders at Premier Sporting Goods were guilty of this when they only measured sales from brick-and-mortar stores. They failed to account for growing online sales because those sales were outside their area of expertise.

They also failed to notice that activities including martial arts were gaining momentum at the expense of traditional American sports like football, baseball, and golf. This shift was causing Premier's business to shrink, and it put the company's future at risk.

Sometimes it takes a traumatic experience to shock leaders out of their comfort zone. This happened when Premier's top retail customer declared bankruptcy. Only then did Jim realize the urgency of his company's situation.

It's important to look beyond our areas of expertise to see what's happening in the broader marketplace. That will help us stay relevant in an ever-changing world.

2. Always Challenge the Status Quo: Often, we continue doing business the same way, and we don't challenge things that have been proven to work in the past. Jim was fortunate when his sponsorship deal with Walt Bigman fell through. It led him to investigate other options and not settle for the way things had been done previously.

We should always question processes that have been in place for years. Often, there are better ways of doing things if we look for other options.

3. Form Alliances: None of us is an expert at everything. Jim formed an alliance with Olivia Whitten, which was instrumental in his success. She had expertise that Jim didn't have, and eventually his alliance with her worked to the advantage of both.

The business world is complicated, and it's important to have as many knowledgeable allies as possible, especially when they're knowledgeable in areas where you aren't.

4. Listen to Everyone: As Jim's wife said, sometimes the quietest people have the most to say. Jim's entire plan shifted when he asked Lisa what she thought. It's important for leaders to ask our people what they think. The best ideas often come from the people who are closest to the work since they can see things that leaders often can't.

5. Ask the Basic Questions: When faced with a business problem, the simplest questions often lead to the best plans. Lisa identified four basic questions that led to the team's successful strategy. Every major initiative should start with basic questions like the ones that Lisa asked:
1. What products should we offer?
2. Who makes the purchasing decisions?
3. Why would people choose those products over others?
4. Where do they buy those products?

6. Define the Customer Journey: In marketing, it's important to understand how customers make their purchase decisions. The Customer Journey framework helps clarify the steps in that process and identifies places where marketers can influence decisions.

When you're working on a marketing campaign, try filling in this Customer Journey framework:

1. Pre-Shop: What triggers the purchase?

2. Shop:
    Awareness: How do customers become aware of new brands?
    Consideration: Where do they get information about brands?
    Purchase: How is the actual purchase made?

3. Post-Shop: What ensures a re-purchase?

7. Gather Insights from Real Consumers: There's no substitute for spending time with your target consumers. You'll always develop a better marketing plan if you spend time with them in their own environment.

If you ask them enough questions, they'll tell you everything you need to know. Then, you just need to change your products and improve your shopping experiences based on their input.

While this seems obvious, think about how much time you actually spend with shoppers and consumers. If you're not interacting with them on a regular basis, do whatever you can to change that.

8. Build Your Media Network: It's important to know exactly who your target audience is, what media options they use, and what content will appeal to them. That will allow you to build marketing campaigns that really connect with them.

We encourage you to use a framework like the one in Section 6 to build your media network. And remember to prioritize the most impactful parts of your media network rather than splitting your resources. Often, focusing on the most influential people in your target audience is better than trying to communicate with everyone.

9. Stop Talking and Start Doing: Jim's friend, Ethan, had some of the best advice in this book. His simple phrase, "Stop talking and start doing" is a reminder that there's no substitute for action.

Too often, we want to analyze every element before making a decision. This leads to needless delays with very little added benefit. Typically, it's better to make a decision quickly, take action, and correct your course based on the outcomes.

10. Rapidly Iterate: The approach that Amy and Ben used was incredibly powerful. They tried things quickly and made adjustments quickly. Using tools like A-B testing, they evaluated different ideas and selected options based on instant input from consumers. This approach allowed them to make real-time changes and accelerate their development process.

This trial-and-error approach is often the best way to get results. As a leader, you need to ensure that your people have permission to try things that might fail. That way, they can be comfortable trying options that could lead to successful changes.

There are many other lessons in this book, so we hope you find content that is useful to you.

We have one request. Please take a few minutes to rate this book and write a review in the online stores where you purchase books. We sincerely want to hear your feedback.

Thanks again, and best wishes in hitting a bullseye with the right products, consumers, and campaign for your organization.

Richard Blazevich & Eric Bishop

Marketing Journey Templates

This section includes templates you can use for your own digital marketing journey. We've included examples from this book along with blank templates for you to complete yourself.

Problems to Solve Statements

As the old saying goes, the first step to recovery is admitting you have a problem. The next step is defining exactly what the problem is. Here are the Premier Sports problems as defined by Jim's wife:

PROBLEMS TO SOLVE:
1. *Products aren't relevant*
2. *Products aren't sold where people shop*

Here are other common problems that organization might have:
- People aren't aware of your brand/company
- Competitors have better quality products
- Expenses are higher than revenue
- Employees aren't motivated

Problems to Solve
_____
_____
_____

The What, Who, Why, and Where

As Lisa explained, it's a good idea to answer a few basic questions before generating solutions to your problems. Here are the answers to these basic questions that the Premier Sports marketing team identified:

1. **What** products should we focus on?

    <u>Martial arts gear</u>

2. **Who** makes the purchasing decisions for those products?

    <u>Martial arts instructors</u>

3. **Why** would people choose those products over others?

    <u>Gear is more comfortable, easier to put on, and stays in place during sparring</u>

4. **Where** do they buy those products?

    <u>Online stores</u>

Use this template to capture your own answers to these key questions for your specific situation:

<u>Key Questions to Ask</u>

1. **What** products should you focus on?

   _____

   _____

2. **Who** makes the purchasing decisions for those products?

   _____

   _____

3. **Why** would people choose your products over others?

   _____

   _____

4. **Where** do they buy those products?

   _____

   _____

Customer Journey

The customer journey captures the steps a shopper takes to decide what to purchase. You can use it to identify ways to influence a shopper's purchase decision. Here's the customer journey that the Premier Sports marketing team identified for martial arts instructors:

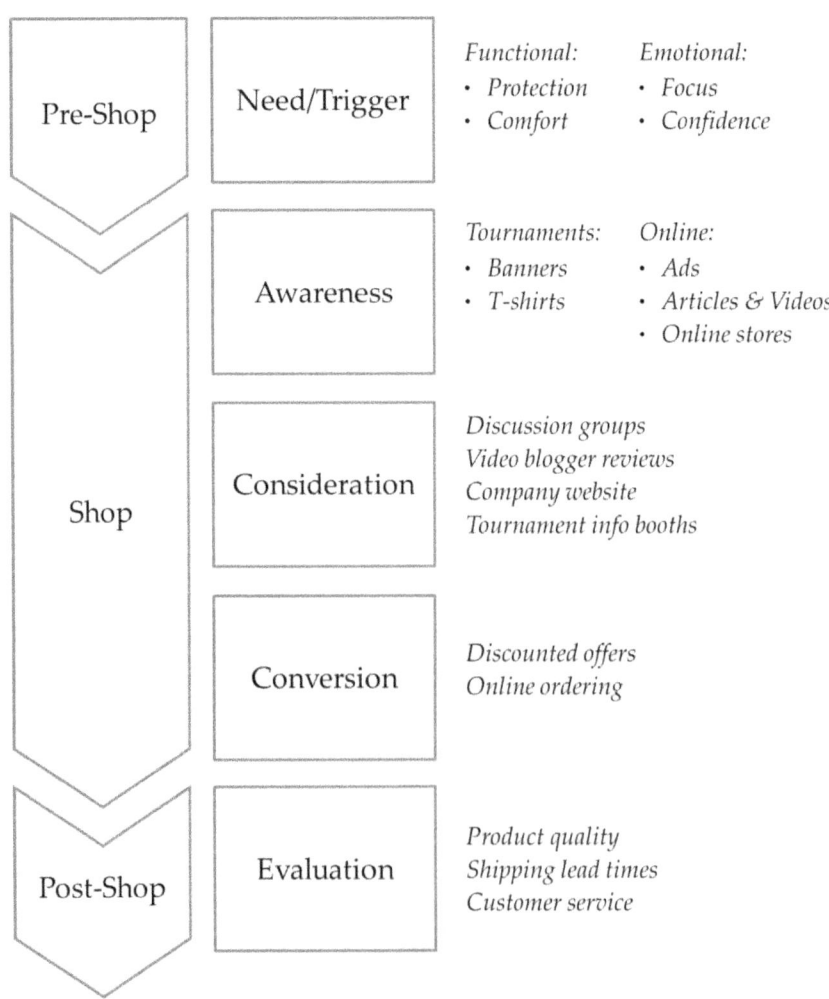

Use this template to capture the customer journey for your organization:

Customer Journey

Stage	Phase	
Pre-Shop	Need/Trigger	_____
Shop	Awareness	_____
Shop	Consideration	_____
Shop	Conversion	_____
Post-Shop	Evaluation	_____

Shopping Funnel

Lisa created this diagram to illustrate ways to guide shoppers to purchase Premier's martial arts gear:

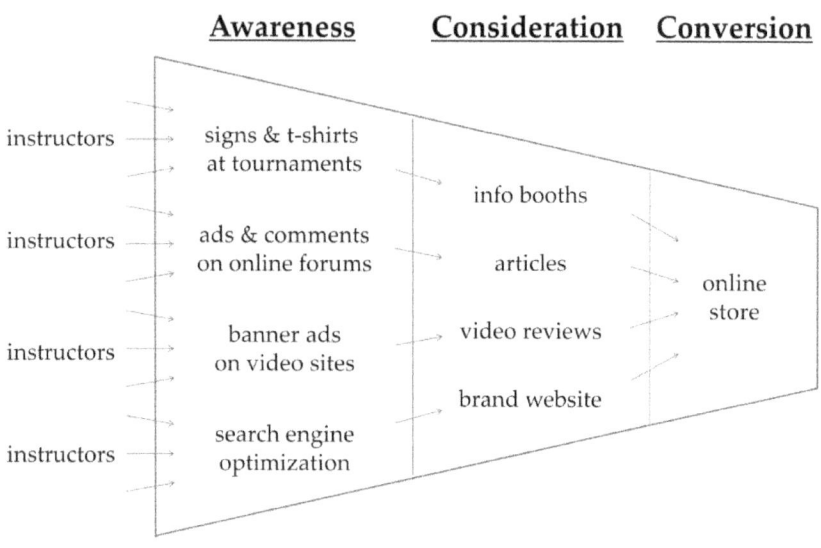

You can create your own shopping funnel for your organization using this template:

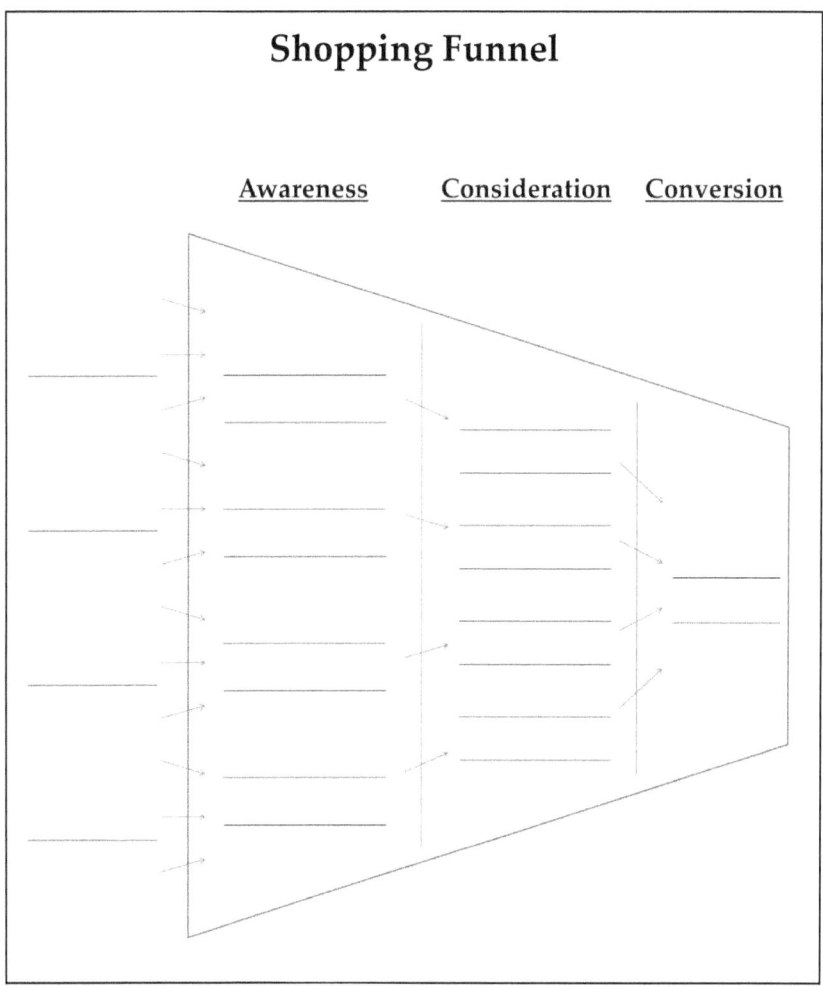

Request-for-Proposal Brief

Here's the brief that the Premier marketing team used to prepare agencies for their agency pitch presentations.

Request-for-Proposal Brief

Thank you for agreeing to meet with us as we look for a new digital agency. We'd like you to give us an overview of your capabilities, examples of your work, and a description of how you'd approach the following project:

Business Challenges:
- Many shoppers are purchasing sporting goods online, but Premier Sporting Goods doesn't have an online presence.
- We'd like to develop a campaign to drive awareness for a new brand of sports equipment that we're launching.
- We'd also like to develop an e-commerce strategy for selling our new products online.

Timing:
- July 20: present agency capabilities
- August 1: finalize agency selection; begin designing campaign
- October 1: finalize campaign elements
- November 1: launch campaign; start selling products online

Presentation Format:
- 30 minutes: present capabilities and examples of your work
- 15 minutes: show us your approach to our business challenges
- 15 minutes: answer questions from our team

To schedule your presentation, please contact Barbara Gaines at bgains@premiersportinggoodscorp.com.

You can use this template whenever you want to explain your objectives and expectations to anyone who is preparing a presentation for you.

Presentation Brief

Thank you for agreeing to meet with us as we look for _____ _____. We'd like you to give us an overview of _____ _____.

Business Challenges or Presentation Objectives: _____
_____
_____

Project Timeline: _____
_____
_____
_____

Presentation Format: _____ minutes for _____
_____ minutes for _____
_____ minutes for _____

To schedule your presentation, contact _____ (person) at _____ (e-mail address or phone number).

Get, To, By, Because Brief

This is a commonly used format for marketing briefs. You can use it to communicate your campaign objectives to your agencies or marketing staff.

Premier Example

GET: *martial arts instructors*
TO: *tell their students to buy Fokasu sparring gear*
BY: *showing them that Fokasu can help their students focus on their lessons*
BECAUSE: *Fokasu delivers the perfect blend of strength, comfort, and consistency*

"Get, To, By, Because" Brief Template

GET: _____
_____ (target audience)

TO: _____
_____ (desired behavior)

BY: _____
_____ (primary message)

BECAUSE: _____
_____ (key benefit)

Design Process

This is the process Amy and Ben from Agile Solutions used to build the online store for Premier Sports. You can use this process to build any website or mobile app.

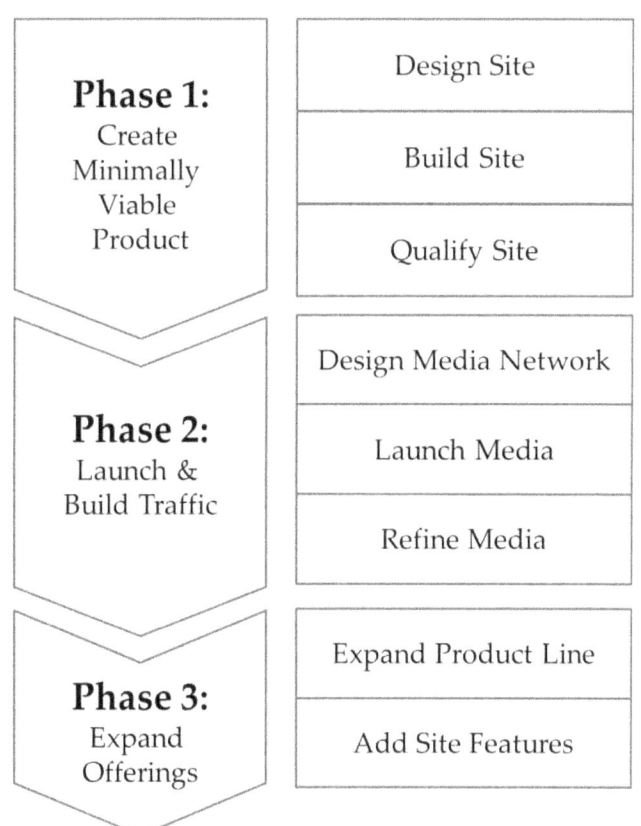

List of Characters

To help you keep track of the role each person plays in this book, here is a list of characters:

Jim Harrison, Chief Marketing Officer
Sarah Harrison, Jim's wife
Jake Harrison, Jim's 15-year-old son
Isabel "Izzy" Harrison, Jim's 10-year-old daughter

Ed Baxter, Chief Executive Officer
Francis Baxter, Chief Financial Officer
Sam Baxter, Chief Sales Officer
Olivia Whitten, Chief Operations Officer

Patrick Feldman, VP of Sports Sponsorships
Barbara Gaines, Director of Sports Sponsorships
Lisa Brimmer, Insights Manager
Mike Reed, Marketing Manager
Jenny Ross, Marketing Analyst

Master Chan, Jake's taekwondo instructor
Ethan Wright, Account Director at Pivot Digital Agency
Cindy Carter, Account Director at Premier's creative agency
Don Marshall, Senior VP of Client Services at Sizzle Media
Amy Brown, Project Director for Agile Solutions
Ben Mathis, Technical Director for Agile Solutions

Acknowledgements

We appreciate everyone who offered assistance and encouragement as we wrote this book. Our wives, Nathalie and Christa, were particularly patient as we spent evenings and weekends working on this project. They also offered useful suggestions for improving the book throughout the process.

Richard's daughter, Sophie Blazevich, who was ten years old when this book was written, collaborated on several sections of the book and added creative suggestions for many of the key characters. She is an incredibly talented writer, and we appreciate her input.

We had two fabulous editors, Trisha Alcisto (www.trishaalcisto.me) and qdmerit (www.fiver.com/qdmerit). Our book cover was designed by a talented graphic artist, Mercedes Piñera (www.behance.net/espacio_M). The dartboard illustration on the cover was provided by ccPixs.com.

The audio version of this book was recorded by Chris Abernathy (www.AbernathyVoice.com). He did an amazing job of bringing this book to life in audio format.

Finally, thank you for taking the time to read this book. We would appreciate it if you enter a rating and a review on the site where you purchased it. We are open to any suggestions you provide for making future versions of this book better.

About the Authors

Richard Blazevich is a senior director of marketing with over 15 years of experience in multinational consumer products companies. He received an MBA with an emphasis in Marketing and Business Strategy from the University of Michigan and a bachelor's degree in Business from Montana State University.

Eric Bishop is a global client director at a multinational technology company. He has 25 years of experience in digital marketing and business strategy. He received his MBA with an emphasis in Marketing and Quantitative Analysis from the University of Cincinnati. He received a bachelor's degree in Computer Science, also from the University of Cincinnati.

Both Richard and Eric have extensive experience leading corporate training programs and recruiting marketing talent from top business schools. They have also been featured speakers at digital marketing conferences and corporate events.

www.ingramcontent.com/pod-product-compliance
Lightning Source LLC
Chambersburg PA
CBHW070248230526
45470CB00002B/520